Baby-led Parenting

Baby-led Parenting

The easy way to nurture, understand and connect with your baby

GILL RAPLEY &
TRACEY MURKETT

Vermilion
LONDON

1 3 5 7 9 10 8 6 4 2

Published in 2014 by Vermilion, an imprint of Ebury Publishing
Ebury Publishing is a Random House Group company

Copyright © Gill Rapley and Tracey Murkett 2014

Gill Rapley and Tracey Murkett have asserted their right to be
identified as the authors of this Work in accordance with
the Copyright, Designs and Patents Act 1988

The Random House Group Limited Reg. No. 954009

Addresses for companies within the Random House Group can be found at
www.randomhouse.co.uk

A CIP catalogue record for this book is available from the British Library

The Random House Group Limited supports the Forest Stewardship
Council® (FSC®), the leading international forest-certification organisation.
Our books carrying the FSC label are printed on FSC®-certified paper. FSC is
the only forest-certification scheme supported by the leading environmental
organisations, including Greenpeace. Our paper procurement policy
can be found at www.randomhouse.co.uk/environment

Printed and bound by CPI Group (UK) Ltd, Croydon, CR0 4YY

ISBN 9780091947545

Cop____ are avail____ ____ ____ ____ bulk orders. Con____ the sales
development team on 020 7840 8487 for more info____ation

To ___ books by ____ fa_____ and register for ____fers visit
www._____co.uk

This boo__ __ a work of _____. ___ ____ names in the ____otations have
_____ _____ privacy of others.

The inform____ ____ in this _____ ____ __ ge____l guidance in
relation to _____ ____ of ____ ____ ____ ____nd not to be
relied on fo____ _____ ____ ____ or other profe____onal advice on
specific ci____ ____ ____ ____ ____ ____. Please con____t ____r GP before
changing, _____ or starting _____ ____ent. So far as the authors are
aware, the _____ given is corre__ __d up to date as at Apr__ 2014. Practice,
laws an____ ____ations all change, ____ the reader should _____ __ up-to-date
professio____ ____ ____ on any such issues. The authors and publishers disclaim,
as far as the law allows, any liability arising directly or indirectly from
the use, or misuse, of the information contained in this book.

Contents

Introduction

When your baby is born, right up until she first begins to crawl, shuffle or toddle away from you to explore, you are the centre of her world. This part of babyhood is sometimes referred to as the 'in arms' phase. It's a period of intense closeness, when her physical and emotional need for you is at its greatest. This is when you get to know her, when you learn how to care for her, discover how to comfort her and how to make her laugh. It's also a period of extraordinary growth, learning and development. The relationships your baby makes during this period are likely to be the most important of her life.

When you are about to start out as a parent, all of this can appear as daunting as it is exciting. Will we know instinctively how bring up our baby? What are the secrets that will help us get it right? How will we avoid the pitfalls that seem to be so common? The sheer volume of information available, and the number of apparently different 'methods' there are to choose from, can seem overwhelming. But you don't need to look very far – you already have your parenting expert on hand, 24/7: *your baby*.

It's often said that babies don't come with an instruction manual – that's because they *are* the manual. Each baby is unique, and each arrives with her own individual temperament and potential. If you give your baby the opportunity, she will show you what she needs and guide you as to the best way to provide it. She can let you know how she likes to be handled, where she prefers to sleep and when she wants to eat. She'll tell you when she's frustrated or scared and show how you can make her feel better. Allowing yourself to be led by your baby is the secret to making her feel safe, loved and confident, and letting her development unfold naturally.

This book will show you how to avoid many of the stumbling blocks that parents commonly encounter, and discover a way of parenting that is intuitive, relaxed and rewarding. It will help you to see life through your baby's eyes and, by learning to understand and communicate with her, to be the best parent you can be for *her*.

Baby-led parenting isn't new. It's a type of parenting that families all over the world have followed for generations, simply because they have found that responding to their baby in a way that keeps her happy makes life more enjoyable for everyone. Yet still today parents are sometimes encouraged – by their families, by health professionals and by the media – to take an approach that is *parent*-led rather than baby-led: one that seeks to control their child's life, even to the extent of deciding how long she should sleep for or how frequently she ought to be cuddled. There is a sense that a baby who doesn't fit easily into a pre-determined pattern is somehow flawed, or that her parents must be doing something wrong, and that this constitutes a problem that can – and should – be fixed. The result is that many parents end up fighting their baby's natural instincts and abilities, preventing her from doing things she is capable of, while at the same time pushing her to do things she can't.

Many of the common assumptions that exist about how babies *should* behave bear little resemblance to how they *do* behave. They are not based on the way real babies develop but on a range of unrealistic expectations, which – even if they were accurate – couldn't possibly apply to every baby. Trying to persuade a baby to comply with them can be a frustrating, uphill battle. Your baby is the only person who really knows if she is hungry, bored or tired. She is the only one to know if the moment is right for her to roll over for the first time, fall asleep by herself, or have her first taste of solid food. So this book won't tell you how long to spend feeding, cuddling or playing with her, when she should be eating three meals a day or when you can expect her to sleep through the night. Instead, *Baby-led Parenting* will help you to recognise your baby's natural rhythms and her changing needs, and to know that you can rely on her as your guide.

Baby-led parenting isn't about allowing your baby to rule your life or always letting her have her own way. It's simply about nurturing, facilitating and supporting her. It means discovering a way of caring for her that fits around her needs and her stage of development, while also working for you, too. It's about understanding the importance of giving her the opportunity to follow her instincts and practise new skills, recognising her readiness for fresh experiences, and knowing how to support rather than interfere as she learns about the world. For many parents, it's the key to more relaxed and rewarding parenting.

The ethos of baby-led parenting is the central theme running through our previous books, *Baby-led Weaning* and *Baby-led Breastfeeding*. This book shows how being baby-led works for pretty much all aspects of parenting, making life easier and more relaxed for everyone. It's the book we both wish we'd had when our children were tiny. It would have taken away some of the confusion of the early days and given us confidence that allowing ourselves to be led by them – which we each learned to do, eventually and to varying degrees – wasn't just lazy (or even slightly irresponsible), but sensible and valuable.

Baby-led Parenting is intended for all parents, whether you plan to combine having children with work or you see yourself as a stay-at-home carer, and whether your baby is breastfed or bottle fed. Most of the text is written for both parents but there are certain sections that are directed more towards the mother, simply because it is she who is most immediately involved in pregnancy, birth and breastfeeding.

Although the focus of the book is the remarkable period when your child is a babe in arms, the principles of baby-led parenting extend far beyond this. Adopting this way of parenting from the start will help you to build a loving relationship with your child, based on a willingness to see things from her perspective and to trust her judgement and capabilities. Of course, you may not be able to follow your baby's lead *all* of the time but we hope our suggestions will help you to stay in touch with her needs whatever the circumstances. By doing this you will create a strong foundation that will enable you to navigate the toddler years, and to continue to nurture and support her throughout her childhood.

Note

Throughout the book, when referring to the baby, we have alternated between *he* and *she*, chapter by chapter, to be fair to both.

1

Baby-led parenting – what it is and why it matters

Baby-led parenting centres around each individual child's needs, personality and abilities. It's about allowing your baby to guide you from the moment he is born, recognising that he is the best person to help you nurture him in a way that is right for *him*, and to adapt as he develops and grows. All of this will help to smooth his transition to the wider world, so that it happens gradually, at his own unique pace.

This chapter explains the basis of the baby-led approach, what makes it so different from some of the alternative ways of bringing up children, and why the extraordinary time when their child is a babe in arms is so important for babies and their parents.

What is baby-led parenting?

Babies' behaviour has evolved over thousands of years to give them the best chance of surviving. Acknowledging babies' innate abilities, their instinctive behaviours, the gradual course of their development, and their natural drive to master new skills is at the heart of baby-led parenting. It's about trusting your baby to know what he needs. It means being in tune with him, listening to what he is telling you, noticing what he is able to do and seeing things from his point of view. It's about empathy, intuition and responsiveness.

The baby-led approach revolves around the need to support babies' **autonomy** and to recognise and respect their **developmental readiness**. Autonomy means babies having an element of control over their lives and being able to decide some things for themselves; developmental readiness acknowledges that each baby develops skills and abilities, and gains emotional maturity, at his own unique pace. Allowing your baby to explore his world, to try out new skills when he is ready, to follow what his body is telling him – for example, by sleeping when he's tired and eating when he's hungry – and to stay close to you for as long as he needs, represents respect for his autonomy *and* his level of development.

Baby-led parenting allows your baby to play an active part in his relationships with you and others. Instead of him simply having to accept what is decided for him and what is done to him, his needs and preferences are taken into consideration. The result is that he is able to shape some of the events that involve him. Being baby-led is an ongoing partnership between you and your baby, in which he shows you what he needs and you work out how best to provide it. It doesn't mean allowing him to control your life – it just means allowing him to have as much control as is possible and reasonable over his *own* life.

> 'Letting my babies lead the way was great. You have to let them choose – you can't just force them to like things they don't. They're people, too! Each one is different and you have to work round that if you want them to be calm and happy.'
>
> *Tina, mother of Ava, 9, and Damon and Jason, 2 years*

All babies reach developmental milestones and acquire new skills in more or less the same order, but in their own time.

They smile, walk and talk when they are ready – there is nothing we can do to hurry them. As long as they are given the opportunity to try out and practise new skills, they'll develop them naturally as they mature. Sometimes parents are told that their baby should have achieved certain things by a particular age, such as sleeping through the night or no longer breastfeeding, but these things don't form part of the normal babyhood sequence of development. Much of this thinking is based on cultural norms, rather than on babies' natural behaviours or up-to-date research. Setting unrealistic goals like these can put enormous pressure on parents to get their baby to comply with others' expectations, and make family life unnecessarily stressful. Baby-led parenting allows you to forget about what your baby *should* do and concentrate instead on what he *can* do, and what works for him and you at any particular time.

What does baby-led parenting mean in practice?

At its simplest, baby-led parenting is about aiming to keep your baby happy, by:

- being open to what he is telling you, and watching and listening for his cues, so that you can work out what he needs and how best to respond to him
- giving him the opportunity to do things that match his stage of development, and adapting as his needs change – for example, keeping him close to you until he lets you know that he is ready to manage on his own
- following his rhythms – learning to recognise his natural cycles and unique patterns, adjusting your routines (as much as possible) to take these things into account, and trusting that he will adapt to *your* rhythms, gradually, as he matures

- empathising with him, seeing things through his eyes, trying to imagine his feelings and finding ways to make even everyday events, such as nappy changing and being dressed, as pleasant and stress-free as possible
- acknowledging that his needs and preferences may change from day to day and week to week, and being ready to accommodate them

In other words, it means watching and listening to what your baby is telling you, to help you to understand his needs and respond to them intuitively.

> 'I try to give Alfie as much love and attention as possible but there's always such a lot of other stuff going on. Trying to make sure the balance is tipped in his favour definitely feels right to me.'
>
> *Rebecca, mother of Alfie, 1 year*

Understanding your baby's needs

Being baby-led is likely to be easier if you can imagine how your baby sees things and try to understand how various different situations might feel to him. This will help you respond to him in a way that meets his needs without feeling frustrated at his demands. The starting point is recognising that most of what *you* know you have found out through experience. For your baby, everything is new and he can find out only gradually, through his own experiences, what is safe – and what (or who) he can rely on.

Your baby needs to be close to you

Babies are born with no memories of past events to draw on. All they have to guide them are their instincts. In this sense, they are no different from babies born 30 years ago – or

30,000. All babies, however rich or poor their parents, and however advanced the technology around them, have the same instincts, needs and urges. These drives exist to help us survive as human beings, and they relate to the environment in which we evolved. The most fundamental of these needs, and the one that can be most difficult to match with 21st-century assumptions about babies, is the need to be close to a familiar person.

At birth, a human baby can do far less for himself than the young of most other mammals because, compared with them, he is born far more immature. This is thought to be an evolutionary adaptation: early humans began to develop bigger brains at around the same time as they began to walk upright, which meant that the mother's pelvis became too narrow for a fully mature baby's head to fit through. So humans evolved to give birth at an earlier stage, when the baby's head is smaller. But this immaturity means that newborn human babies are extremely vulnerable. A young baby cannot get himself out of harm's way or regulate his temperature, and he can't find his own food. For most of history human beings lived in an environment in which a baby left alone for even a short time was at risk of being eaten by a predator or dying of excess heat or cold – or simply (because breastmilk is digested very quickly) of going hungry. All of this means that, as humans, we evolved to carry our young with us, rather than leaving them for long periods in a den or a nest.

In traditional societies the person carrying the baby is most likely to be his mother. It's the baby's mother who is his first place of safety – she provides him with warmth, protection and nourishment, right from the moment of birth, and he is already familiar with her voice, her smell and her heartbeat from his time in the womb. This is why newborns instinctively want to stay close to their mother. And, because babies' limited experience of the world means they have no sense of space or time, their instinct also tells them that they need to be within touching (or at least sniffing) distance of her, night and day, if they are to feel truly safe.

Of course, in the 21st century, post-industrialised world the risks to a newborn baby aren't quite the same, but our babies don't know this. Without his mother close, the newborn is likely to feel frightened. Unlike an ape baby, who can cling to his mother's fur, or a baby deer, who can follow her if she moves away, a human baby has to rely on his mother to keep him with her – so he'll do everything he can to get her attention and make her want to protect him. Your baby can't come and find you if you are apart from him. If he can't see you or smell you, he doesn't know that you are nearby and that you will return – and he doesn't know that he will be safe until you do. He will learn these things over time but, for now, all he can do is try to call you back. If your response isn't fairly swift, or if you offer no soothing words or touch while he waits for you to pick him up, he won't know he's been heard and he is likely to become distressed.

Babies (don't just) need their mother

A mother and her newborn baby are sometimes referred to as a 'dyad' – two units so closely linked and interdependent that they are regarded as one. Indeed, as far as the baby is concerned they *are* one (he won't even begin to understand that he is a separate person until he is at least three months old). This new pairing is fragile; it needs to be protected and supported – which is where the father (or other supporter) comes in. His primary role is to safeguard this fledgling relationship, nourishing it and allowing it to grow. His own relationship with the baby is important, but in the beginning it's the baby's connection with his mother that takes centre stage.

Seeing things from your baby's perspective, and understanding how your presence reassures and comforts him, will help you to respond to him in a way that is baby-led. Trusting him to know what he needs – even if you can't always work out why he needs it – is the key to allowing him to guide you.

> 'I didn't really understand how good it is for babies to be close all the time when Asha was tiny. I wish I had. I carried Sammi everywhere in a sling from day one. I loved having him close to me and being able to smell him. There's nothing like the smell of a newborn baby's skin! He's very calm and secure in himself now – I'm sure that early closeness had something to do with it.'
>
> Jenni, *mother of Asha-Mei, 3 years, and Sammi-Li, 20 months*

Your baby needs comfort

Feelings and emotions are more than just thoughts inside our head – they trigger a physical reaction that involves our whole body. Each time we feel happy, sad, scared or anxious, hormones are released into our bloodstream, affecting our pulse rate and breathing and determining how we respond to those around us. Pleasurable feelings trigger the release of hormones such as oxytocin and dopamine, which make us feel and act lovingly towards others, relax us and give us a 'high'. Stress and fear, on the other hand, trigger hormones such as adrenaline and cortisol, which prepare us to respond to danger. In general, calming hormones have a stronger effect, so that when we are comforted our stress hormone levels drop rapidly. This process is known as regulation.

Most adults are capable of recognising when danger has passed, or of finding ways to cheer themselves up when they are feeling miserable – in other words, they can *self-regulate*. Babies and young children can't do this because they aren't able to rationalise or control how they feel. They can't 'think up' the release of calming hormones when they are stressed or afraid; they need comfort from someone else for this to happen. Without the counteracting effect of calming hormones the levels of stress hormones take much longer to subside.

'It can be hard to trust your instincts, but I thought: if they cry they need me. Even if it's just comfort – so what?'

Dawn, mother of Layla, 5, and Ruby, 2 years

Babies can't wait

Parents who respond to their baby swiftly when he needs them can sometimes be told they are making a rod for their own back, and that if they don't make him wait he'll never learn to be patient. This really doesn't make sense. Patience requires an awareness of time, a sense of other people's needs and the ability to think things through. These don't develop until well into childhood. A baby whose requests for help don't get a response will at first try harder to make himself heard and understood. How long he keeps trying depends on his personality and on his experience so far, but eventually, if nobody comes, he may well conclude that his attempts at communication are not working and decide to give up trying. But this isn't the same as patience.

If, like most little children, your newborn seems to need a lot of attention it doesn't mean he's destined to always be demanding; it's just that he doesn't yet have the experience or understanding to enable him to wait. Responding quickly to his requests will help him to gain confidence in his ability to communicate with you and to learn, gradually, that he can rely on you to listen. This is the beginning of trust, which is the basis for patience, and of developing an awareness of others' feelings. In fact, research shows that children who have had this sort of nurturing grow up better able to socialise (and to learn) than those who have had less responsive care.

A baby who is not comforted when he cries will eventually settle. Often, he is described as having 'self-soothed'. However, babies can't regulate their own emotions in this way, and research suggests that, even though he has stopped crying, the baby's stress hormone levels may still be quite high. By contrast, babies who are comforted whenever (or almost whenever) they are upset have been shown to have higher levels of beneficial, calming hormones – not only just after a bout of crying but as a general rule.

You won't always be able to make your child's distress better – all babies cry sometimes, and it's impossible to know what's wrong every time – but by acknowledging his feelings and soothing him when he's upset, even if you can't solve the problem, you will help him learn to deal with stress effectively, which, in turn, will help to provide him with a long-term buffer against the ups and downs of life.

> 'When my mum was a baby, my gran was told to leave her to cry, unless she needed feeding. She said it broke her heart to do it. She's really envious of me being "allowed" to carry Ben everywhere and amazed at how little he cries.'
>
> *Gaby, mother of Ben, 5 months*

Your baby needs to feel safe

Feeling safe is important for all of us. It isn't just about knowing we're okay *now*; it's about having a deeper sense of security that gives us the courage to explore new things. Anything unknown or unpredictable is much less scary when looked at from somewhere we feel safe; the more secure a baby feels the more free he will be to learn, and to enjoy new experiences.

The place where a young baby feels safest is in his parent's arms – keeping your baby close to you will help him to get the most out of what's going on around him.

New people and new places can be especially frightening for babies – and it's easy to forget that what is familiar to you may not be to your baby. If it's something he hasn't encountered before, he'll cope with it much better if you're holding him than if he can't feel you near him. Until he can move away and come back to you by himself he is dependent on you to keep him close. Even later on, when he *can* crawl across the room, he will still need you to be available – and he will look for you in the place where he left you. Your baby is the best judge of his need for you; giving him a secure base from which to size up new situations will allow him to decide when he is ready to explore them.

> 'I try to treat Bethany with as much respect as I would an older child or my partner. I think some parents are scared to do that in case they have no control. But I've found the opposite is true. She's not afraid of us. Now she's older, if she spills something, she won't hide it – she'll just come and tell us. She's definitely not wild!'
>
> *Kate, mother of Bethany, 2 years*

Your baby needs opportunities to develop his skills

Babies develop new skills gradually. Although your baby's ability to do something new may seem to appear overnight (one day he can't smile, grab his toes or say 'Dadda', and the next, he can), in reality, he's been leading up to that moment for a long time. For example, it will take him four or five months of trial, error and increasing muscle strength and co-ordination to discover the various combinations of movements that result in rolling over (as well as all those that don't!).

Babies don't need anyone to nudge their development along, but they are reliant on their parents to provide them with opportunities that will give them the best chance of developing at the pace that is right for them. For example, to discover how to roll over, they need enough space and time to experiment – even if it's just when they're in bed or having their nappy changed. And they need to practise and consolidate new skills before they are ready to move on. Each set of movements is built on the last, and involves lots of testing and refinement. Allowing babies to progress in their own time means they are always building on a strong foundation, whereas pushing them to go faster can result in a later skill being less reliable than it should be. It's a bit like an older child trying to do wheelies on his bike before he's learnt to start and stop safely. There aren't any shortcuts – babies need to practise the basics first, and move on only when they feel ready.

Being baby-led means allowing your baby to extend his range of abilities and have a go at whatever seems to interest him, rather than deciding for him what the next thing should be. It can be as simple as giving him time to explore his fingers or toes, or to touch and play with food. Mostly, it's just a matter of sharing your life with your baby, noticing what he is interested in – and not limiting his experiences or preventing him from trying things because you don't think he's ready. He'll naturally want to look at and handle a variety of objects, so as to develop hand–eye co-ordination and dexterity; to move his limbs to increase strength and agility; and to be talked and listened to, face to face, so he can learn to use facial expressions and speech. Letting him show you what he is capable of, and trusting him to do things in his own time, is the best way to ensure that his development happens at the ideal speed for him.

Developing true independence

The ultimate aim of bringing up a child is sometimes seen as enabling him to achieve independence. This means, literally, having no need of anyone else. This is fine if, like a male tiger cub, the baby is destined to live a lone existence. But it's not appropriate for most people, who need and want to interact with others as part of family groups and communities. Some level of dependence on others is normal and desirable – if we were all totally independent, we wouldn't need clubs, teams or online forums – and most adults are happy to turn to family and friends for some things, even if it's just for comfort when they are feeling down.

Babies and children need support, reassurance and comfort to achieve the right balance of dependence and independence. Those who are pushed to manage on their own before they are ready may appear very independent but this type of independence isn't the same as true self-reliance. In the long term, the need to 'put on a brave face' can mean they find it difficult to ask for help when they need it, or to accept help when it *is* offered. On the other hand, when a baby's abilities are not trusted, or his preferences are disregarded and he is *prevented* from doing things for himself, he may become wary of trusting his own judgement and end up deferring to others in every situation, meaning that the development of true independence is disrupted.

Giving your baby help as and when he shows you he needs it, and trusting him to know both his capabilities and his limitations, is the best way to help him develop a healthy level of self-belief and confidence. As he grows up, this type of support will give him a better chance of being self-reliant when necessary, but able to ask for, and receive, help if it's needed – and to recognise when others need *his* help.

'I was raised in a very gentle way but I didn't realise how much it had influenced me until I had Evelyn. I think it's made everything much easier for me compared to my husband, who was brought up very differently. I seem to have more patience than him. I want Evelyn to be that way if she has children.'

Cheryl, mother of Evelyn, 2 years

What's wrong with being parent-led?

Baby-led parenting isn't new but it is very different from some other approaches. Following your baby's lead is more or less the opposite approach from those that emphasise more parental control, and which usually involve devising or adopting a pre-determined schedule. Designating times for feeding, sleeping and playing can work for some parents (in the short term, at any rate), but parent-led approaches like this rarely take into account the baby's developmental stage, his individuality, or the fact that his (and his parents') needs and moods change from day to day.

In practice, many parents find trying to follow a schedule leads them into battle with their baby. This is because, at least some of the time, they are likely to have to override his needs – for example, by trying to get him to sleep when he isn't tired, or persuading him to wait when he is trying to tell them he is hungry. Parents who have tried scheduled parenting often say they spend a lot of time comforting their baby while they wait until the 'right' time to give him what he wants.

'Sometimes in the early days I just thought I wasn't very good at being a mum because I hadn't managed to get Lulu to settle in a cot or to go to sleep when she was supposed to, and I fed her whenever she asked. But I just couldn't go against what she seemed to want – I didn't want her to cry. I felt bad about it until I met some mums who did similar things and realised it was okay.'

Annie, mother of Lulu, 2 years

Babies don't need to be persuaded or 'trained' to do things that are completely natural activities. They know when they are tired or hungry and their survival instinct means they will do their best to communicate that need. Trying to persuade a baby to wait when his body tells him he needs something *now* can be exhausting. Fixed schedules also have the potential to seriously disrupt breastfeeding (see page 116) and to interfere with sleep (see page 138). Many families report, too, that they struggle with the lack of flexibility inherent in a schedule. For example, a long car journey or day spent visiting friends can easily interfere with a pre-planned time-table for eating and sleeping.

A scheduled approach can seem like one way to negotiate the uncertainty and apparent chaos of the first few weeks or months with a new baby. However, the unpredictability of the newborn period doesn't last long. Most parents who allow themselves to be led by their baby's needs, rather than by a schedule, find their baby's own pattern inevitably emerges. This allows life to become more predictable naturally, with a rhythm that is right for the baby and his needs at the time.

Babies change as they get older, and so do their needs. Unlike a schedule devised by someone else, your baby's own pattern can and will evolve with him, at his own unique pace, allowing you to adapt to the inevitable changes gradually and intuitively. Listening to him, and making sure he has what he tells you he needs, won't spoil him or prevent you making decisions for him when you have to; it will simply allow you to grow *with* him, cementing a bond that will continue to become stronger throughout his childhood.

'Before I had babies I had no idea there were so many different approaches to looking after them. When I was pregnant I met up with friends who followed schedules with their babies but they seemed really stressed trying to keep to a timetable. And Sienna seems to be constantly changing – it must be really hard to be that rigid. For me, being flexible makes it easier to cope with all the changes.'

Rachael, mother of Sienna, 7 months

Key points

- Baby-led parenting respects a baby's autonomy and his developmental readiness. It's about giving your baby the opportunity to make choices for himself, when he is ready.
- The baby-led approach supports and encourages a foundation of trust and a strong bond between parent and baby.
- The most fundamental need of a newborn baby – after warmth and food – is to be close to another human being.
- Babies can't regulate their emotions by themselves and they don't know how to wait; they need someone to comfort them when they're upset.
- Babies need to feel safe in order to have the confidence to manage new experiences. Young babies feel safest when they're in their parent's arms.
- Babies need the opportunity to use their abilities and develop new skills at their own pace, when they are ready.
- True independence can't be forced – it needs to be supported and nurtured. Baby-led parenting helps a baby to develop confidence in his abilities.

2

Becoming a parent – expectations and plans

Part of expecting a baby is imagining what life will be like when she arrives, especially if she's your first. As you watch and feel her moving and growing you'll probably find yourself musing about who she will take after, how she'll behave and what kind of parent you'll be. This chapter is about this period of anticipation; it looks at where our expectations about being a parent come from and at how you can start your unique parenting journey even before your baby is born.

Our expectations about babies

The daydreams you have when you are expecting your baby are likely to have their roots in a combination of your own experiences as a child, what you see other parents doing and what you have heard, seen or read throughout your life about babies and how they behave. Nowadays, many of us grow up in small families with no extended family nearby, and it's not unusual to reach adulthood with little practical experience of caring for a baby – or even of holding one. But even if we have had lots of practice at looking after babies, what we can't anticipate, with our first baby at any rate, is how becoming a parent will change us. It's almost impossible to imagine in advance how emotions we have never experienced

21

will affect our decisions and the way we see things. Parenting comes from the heart as well as the head, and many parents find their ideas get turned upside down once they meet their own baby. For all these reasons, most find that the reality of life with a young baby is very different from the way they had imagined it would be.

'The moment I became a mum I became a different person. My perception of *everything* changed.'

Rianne, mother of Emma, 5, Harry, 3 years, and Jack, 6 months

One of the hardest things to envisage, especially when you're expecting your first child, is just how much your baby will depend on you, night and day. Many parents-to-be worry about how they'll cope with this level of need; others are confident the arrival of a baby won't change things all that much. Most simply assume there'll be a bit of trial and error while they find their way. Whether or not you actively seek advice, you'll probably find it hard to avoid encountering other people's ideas on how best to bring up a baby. However, it's worth bearing in mind that at least some of what you will read and hear is likely to be based on misconceptions about how babies develop. Plus, of course, your baby is unique – and, since no one has yet been a parent to *her*, no one can have all the answers. Recognising where your own expectations come from and understanding the root of some of the ideas and advice that you are likely to come across will help you navigate your way through the inevitable surprises and frustrations of becoming a parent.

'Alex didn't do anything I expected. I thought my maternity leave would be a bit of time for myself; I'd read nice books and relax while the baby fed and slept peacefully. But he only wanted to feed and sleep in my arms – he just wouldn't let me put him down.'

Marie, mother of Alex, 4 years, and Freya, 18 months

How society views babies' behaviour

New parents are sometimes asked whether or not their baby is a 'good baby'. This comes from an old-fashioned but pervasive view that babies are capable of either good or bad behaviour: babies who appear content are considered to be good, whereas those who seem to need a lot of attention are thought of as difficult. But it's normal for most healthy babies to protest, for example, if they are not close enough to their parents to feel safe (see page 8) or if they are feeling bored or tired. A baby who is too easy-going can miss out on the attention and company that all babies thrive on.

A 'good' baby is often seen as a sign of a good parent, and mothers and fathers can feel under enormous pressure to get their baby to conform to what they (or others) believe is acceptable. This can include trying to make her behave in ways that are widely considered desirable but have no real basis in natural child development. For example, parents may be told that their baby should be sleeping through the night by a certain age, or be content to have naps in a room alone; that she should be able to amuse herself with her toys; or be happy to feed only at set times. Mostly, these are unrealistic expectations. They are the result of confusion between physical milestones – like smiling, rolling over and walking (which will happen spontaneously when the time is right) – and behaviours that are linked to emotions and self-confidence, which are not time-bound.

When their baby behaves in ways that are not what they – or others – expect, many parents feel they have to find ways to change things. They can easily imagine there must be something wrong with her – or with them – and that they should be able to sort it out. And yet, the chances are their baby's behaviour is perfectly normal. Babies know what they need to do, and trying to change their behaviour without addressing what's causing it rarely works. Looking at things from your baby's point of view, and forgetting about your own and other people's expectations, can help make sense of what she does, so that you feel more confident to respond to her intuitively.

> 'Sometimes people will tell me to do things in a different way, and I'll maybe try it in front of them or tell them I'm going to try it, but then I'll just go back to what we were doing before. I know what works for my baby and it isn't necessarily the same as whatever worked for theirs.'
>
> Louise, mother of Skye, 7 months

Babies don't just want to feed, or play, or be held – they need these things. When they don't have what they need to feel safe and loved, they try to tell us – and they can quickly become distraught if nobody listens. Some people see a baby's normal, instinctive attempts to elicit a response from her carers as manipulative or demanding, as if the baby is trying to trick her parents into giving her what she wants. The problem is that this thinking doesn't fit with how babies' minds actually work. Babies live in the present. They are incapable of thinking ahead, or of understanding the consequences of their (or anyone else's) actions. And they can't imagine how anyone else feels. When your baby is in distress she knows only how *she* feels, now – she can't help the effect her needs have on you and, as we've seen (page 12), she isn't able to wait until a more convenient time.

> 'It's impossible to grasp the commitment needed before you have babies – it shouldn't be underrated. I'm no stranger to hard work but the sheer workload involved in kids is a whole new ball game.'
>
> Simon, father of Joshua, 4 years, and Felix, 6 months

It can be hard to ignore the common misconceptions about how babies think and why they behave as they do, especially when previous generations of parents had this sort of information drummed into them. Babies' temperaments vary:

some are naturally very easy-going, while others need more in the way of stimulation or reassurance. Taking time to understand your baby, and what your instincts tell you she needs, will help you to be confident that what you are doing is right for her.

Your expectations of yourself as a parent

Most of what we think of as instinctive parenting responses aren't actually instinctive at all – they're something we've absorbed as we've grown up. We are programmed to be attracted to our babies, to fall in love with them and to want to respond to them. But how we respond is largely dependent on the sort of parenting we've seen around us, the parenting styles our friends adopt, what we see in the media, and the sort of care we experienced ourselves.

For many people, the way their parents cared for them is what feels 'normal', even if they can't describe it. When they are about to become parents themselves, some assume they'll follow what their parents did, without even thinking about it, while others start to scrutinise their childhood experiences and question whether they want to act the same way, or differently, towards their own child. Many find that their partner has very different ideas, based on his or her own experiences.

'I had a lot of very strong opinions about what sort of parent I was going to be, even as a child. I was breastfed for ages and was never smacked – I was shouted at sometimes, but Mum says she regretted it. I thought all that was the normal way until at secondary school I realised that childhood was very different for many kids. I was determined I was going to do things in a similar way to my mum but it took me a while to persuade my husband that the sort of discipline *he*'d experienced wasn't what we wanted for our kids.'

Jo, mother of Madeleine, 2 years

Whatever your thoughts about the sort of parent you want to be, it may be worth reflecting on the way you were cared for because this is likely to be your default response, especially in stressful situations. So, if the care you received was largely positive, you'll probably feel most comfortable responding in a nurturing way to your baby. But if you had mainly negative experiences, you may find your immediate reaction is sometimes less caring. However, these learnt responses aren't set in stone; they can be unlearned. Giving yourself plenty of time to hold your baby and listen to what she is trying to tell you will help you to see life through her eyes and work out what she needs you to do.

For some people, taking a closer look at their parents' approach to parenting is affirming, but for others it is unsettling. Making a conscious decision to mirror what your parents did may well draw you closer to them and make you want to involve them in your children's upbringing. On the other hand, choosing to reject some or all of the elements of the way you were cared for, and deciding to behave differently with your own child, may make things uncomfortable for both you and them, and may lead to feelings of criticism and hurt. It can be helpful to remember that, at whatever point in time, most parents have their children's interests at heart and want very much to do what's best for them. It's also important to recognise that most new parents are heavily influenced by the child-rearing practices they see around them and it can be hard to swim against the tide. Plus, of course, we all make decisions based on the information available to us at the time – and we all make mistakes.

Of course, not everyone knows how they were cared for as a baby. Your parents may not be alive, you may not be in contact with them or they may simply not be able to remember what they did, or be willing to talk about it. So although you'll have memories of the care you received as an older child, and that will offer some clues, you may not be able to uncover the details of how you were cared for in your earliest years. This may leave you feeling slightly uncertain about what you are supposed to do – or it may leave you *more* free to make your own decisions, or to decide just to trust your baby.

> 'My mum died a few years before Holly was born. I'd never really asked her much about what she did when we were all babies – I just wasn't interested until I wanted my own children. I asked my dad how long I was breastfed for but he had no idea. He just said: "Well, I expect your mother stopped whenever you are supposed to stop." I remember feeling a bit lost when I first had Holly, and really missing my mum. One day when Holly was crying, I held her close and started patting her bottom rhythmically to comfort her, and saying: "There, there," over and over. It suddenly felt so right. I'm sure it was a really deep memory of what my mother did with me. I felt much more confident after that; I felt as though I knew how to *be* with my baby.'
>
> *Stella, mother of Holly, 7 months*

The legacy of past generations

How you were brought up is likely to have been influenced both by how your parents were raised and by the prevailing childcare ethos at the time you were a baby. Although there have always been parents who have been more or less responsive to their children, and some parenting books that encouraged this, for over a century the prevailing advice has been distinctly *parent*-led, rather than baby-led. This may well have influenced your childhood, and in turn what you feel parenting involves.

Recent generations of parents were often advised not to 'indulge' their infants by picking them up and comforting them, which effectively meant fighting their baby's needs for closeness and their own instinctive urges for nurturing. For instance, from the 1930s to the 1960s, separation was usually enforced almost as soon as the baby was born, with newborns taken away so that their mothers could rest, and brought back for feeds only every four hours. Babies usually spent their first nights in the hospital nursery, where they would be bottle fed by a nurse, and their mothers were instructed to maintain scheduled feeds when they got home. This meant that babies were left to cope without their mothers for long periods (and their chances of being breastfed long term were severely reduced, too – see page 103).

Torn between their own urge to hold their baby close and the weight of common opinion that to do so would spoil her, many parents found these strict regimes difficult and distressing to implement. Eventually, in the 1970s and 1980s, gentler ways of caring for babies started to gain ground (although it took another decade or two for hospital practices to catch up). However, many of the older ideas remained ingrained and, in more recent years, more rigid approaches have once again become popular, even though there is now research that suggests such approaches are not good for babies.

The impact of their own experiences can sometimes make it difficult for grandparents to know quite how to support their grown-up children if they decide to do things another way. For example, if they were warned they would spoil their babies if they picked them up too much, and were advised to feed them 'by the clock', it can be hard for them to understand parents who want to keep their baby close to them all the time, and feed them as often as they want. Many grandparents, though, are open to new ideas and may remember rejecting elements of their own parents' childcare methods when they had their children.

'I hated leaving my first son to cry – he sounded so desperate and I really had to force myself to ignore him. I was told I'd spoil him if I went to him when it wasn't time. It was a bit easier with the second and third because I'd decided I could be a bit more flexible.

But I didn't dare pick them up every time, just in case everyone was right.'

Betty, mother of three boys born in the 1950s and grandmother of seven

Modern challenges

Twenty-first-century lifestyles can make it difficult for parents to implement their preferred style of parenting. For example, rent and mortgages based on a double-income household can put new families under pressure financially when it comes to questions of maternity/paternity leave and whether both parents need to do paid work. Many women today have their first child at a later stage in their life than their mothers did. They may be established in a career or job and find it difficult to imagine how they will make their new role as a mother run smoothly alongside their working life (for more on this, see page 218).

Our concepts of fatherhood have changed, too. A generation or two ago, hands-on fathers were still a novelty and many men struggled to adapt to the concept; most were happy for childcare to be an almost exclusively female domain, with their own role that of more distant family breadwinner. Today, although some fathers work from home and others are full-time dads, many still spend long hours away from their families. The majority are not content to see their children only when they're tucked up in bed or at weekends. All of this can create tension between partners when they are faced with the challenge of working together to bring up the next generation.

Finding your own way

Talking with your partner about different ways of caring for babies and small children is an important part of preparing for parenting as a couple. Sharing some of your childhood experiences will give you a sense of how similar or different your upbringing was, while discussing how you see other parents reacting to their children's behaviour will help you discover whether your ideas for how such situations should be handled coincide or clash. There's no need to agree on everything – and it can help later if your ideas aren't too fixed just yet anyway – the important thing is to be receptive to alternative ways of doing things, and to be ready to take your baby's wishes into account. If you don't have a partner, you may find it helpful to talk with a friend or relative who has had children. Even if they won't be around every day to share your parenting decisions, it may be useful to have them as a sounding board to help you discover the sort of parent you want to be.

'When I was pregnant with Ellie we wanted to make sure she wouldn't be spoiled, so we said we wouldn't pick her up with the first cry, would make sure she went to her bed on time, and so on. But once she was born I couldn't do those things. It felt as if I was going against nature and that I was creating a barrier between us. And now I think it's lovely for them all to have known such unconditional love.'

Leanne, *mother of Ellie, 6, Joseph, 2 years, and Bayley, 10 months*

Pregnancy – the start of parenting

Pregnancy is a time for looking ahead but it's also a time for starting to get to know your baby. Some parents begin to make a connection with their baby as soon as the pregnancy is suspected or confirmed; for others, feeling their baby move or seeing her image on a scan monitor triggers the sense that this is a real person, waiting to meet them.

From very early in pregnancy a baby is responding to and learning about the world outside her mother's body. She tastes flavours from her foods in the amniotic fluid that surrounds her, and she can sense the difference between light and dark.

But it's noises and movement she responds to most obviously. Many parents find themselves massaging the bump, and singing, talking and even reading stories to their baby, and research shows that babies seem to recognise, later, these same stories and tunes, and that they are calmed by them.

Many mothers-to-be feel enormously protective over their unborn child. Some spontaneously stroke their pregnant belly if there is a loud noise, as if calming their baby, often without realising they are doing it, and scans show that babies in the womb do indeed appear to cry in response to sudden loud noises. Research also shows that the heartbeat of a baby in the womb changes when she hears her mother's voice, and that unborn babies are able to move their limbs in time to music. Mothers of twins or multiples, or several single children, often comment on how differently each baby behaved while in the womb, and how their responses seemed to be a forecast of the character traits they showed once they were born.

> 'When I was pregnant with the boys I didn't feel connected until we had the first scan; that's when we found out it was twins – it was so exciting. And when they started to move, Markos was quiet and calm and Marios was moving around all the time, more like my first child, Julia, had. So I always knew they had different personalities.'
>
> *Zina, mother of Julia, 11, and Marios and Markos, 3 years*

If you want to connect with your unborn baby but are finding it difficult, visualising her inside the womb, and keeping track of her week-to-week development (online, with a phone app or using a book), along with massaging, singing and talking directly to her, rather than just about her, may help – as will using her name (if you've chosen it), or giving her a nickname. The first few times you talk out loud to her may feel a bit strange, but the more you do it, the easier it will be. And it doesn't matter what you talk about, or what music or stories you choose – she'll almost certainly enjoy whatever *you* like.

Antenatal depression

Depression during pregnancy (also known as prenatal depression) is less talked about than depression following a birth but it is a reality for a significant minority of women. Antenatal depression can interfere with the connection the mother feels with her unborn baby, and it may predispose her to postnatal depression (see page 214). If, while you're pregnant, you experience symptoms such as chronic anxiety, guilt or extreme fatigue, or you find yourself low-spirited or crying most of the time, talk to your midwife or GP.

Parents who are expecting their second baby can have very mixed feelings during the pregnancy. Having fallen in love with one child some find it difficult to imagine feeling the same way towards another one. They may wonder how their love can stretch that far and may be frightened of being disloyal to their firstborn. The doubt usually vanishes once the new baby is born – most mothers and fathers find they fall in love all over again, with each child they have.

'I thought I'd never love another child as much as I loved Jasmine – I just couldn't imagine it. Everybody thought I must be looking forward to the second one but the closer it got the more scared I was. I needn't have worried. As soon as I saw Josh it all fell into place and I realised he made us complete. Love is limitless – it just keeps expanding to accommodate new people. You don't have to chuck the old ones out!'

Sasha, mother of Jasmine, 3 years, and Joshua, 6 months

Planning for meeting your baby

The last few months of pregnancy are a great time to think about the practicalities of how you want to welcome your baby into the world and what will make it easier for you to start getting to know each other. Writing things down can be a useful way to clarify your ideas about what you'd *like* to happen, whether it's during labour, in the first few hours after the birth, or during your baby's hospital stay. For example, you may want to consider who you want to be present, both at the birth and in the first few hours afterwards (many parents find having visitors too soon distracting). Of course, it's impossible to predict exactly what's going to happen, but

Ideas for your birth plan

Here are a few of the things you may want to discuss with your midwife in advance of your baby's birth, so that you know what is likely to happen and what alternative options are available:

- *Medical interventions and drugs:* Some drugs given to the mother in labour (including those used in epidural pain relief) can make babies abnormally sleepy for the first few days, which can interfere with their instinctive behaviours and may delay the beginning of bonding.
- *Cutting the cord:* Many midwives and obstetricians now delay cutting the umbilical cord until it has stopped pulsating. This allows the baby a gentler transition to breathing on her own and ensures she gets her full quota of iron-rich blood.
- *Skin-to-skin contact:* You will almost certainly be offered the chance to spend some time with your baby lying on your chest, with her skin touching yours, immediately after the birth, but you may want to discuss beforehand some ways of making sure that this first hour or so is as uninterrupted as possible (see page 47).

See Chapter 3 for more on how to make the most of welcoming your baby.

having a written birth plan will give the midwives and other staff a guide to your preferences, and provide something to refer to if things start to happen fast.

Working on a birth plan also helps mothers to think ahead to some of the more basic details, such as what to take into hospital and what to wear during labour (or during a planned caesarean operation) – skin-to-skin contact with a new baby is generally easier to manage in a jacket-type pyjama top, loose cardigan or shirt (or a back-to-front hospital gown) than in a T-shirt or nightie. If you have a choice of where to have your baby, finding out which of your local hospitals are accredited as Baby Friendly (as part of the UNICEF UK Baby Friendly Initiative; see 'Sources of Information and Support', page 230) or have one or more members of staff who specialise in breastfeeding, may help you make your decision. A Baby Friendly environment will mean you can be confident you'll be supported to breastfeed from the beginning.

Most couples find that if they discuss the things they'd like to happen (as far as circumstances allow), both during labour and in the following hours or days, the mother can feel more free to concentrate on giving birth.

Planning for the first few weeks

The first few weeks of your baby's life are the beginning of building a secure, baby-led relationship with her; thinking ahead to this special time will help you make the most of it. Many parents make a conscious decision to have a two-week 'babymoon' (see Chapter 4), to give themselves a chance to recover from the upheaval of birth, get breastfeeding up and running, and start getting to know their baby. The idea is to keep the intrusion of everyday life to a minimum, while surrounding yourself with people who will offer you the sort of support you really need. The last few weeks of pregnancy

Preparing older children

The arrival of a new baby is an enormous event for older children in the family, and the younger a child is, the more likely it is to be unsettling for him. Many parents find that making sure their child's expectations are as realistic as possible beforehand can help things go more smoothly when the baby arrives. Talking about what newborn babies actually do (and don't do), and explaining how much a new baby needs her mummy (just as the older child did when *he* was little) can be useful starting points. Looking together at photos or videos of the older child as a newborn can help, as can sharing books about the arrival of a new baby. Meeting young babies – perhaps at a friend's house or a parent–baby group – and talking about what they are doing (usually lots of feeding, sleeping and being cuddled) is another way to build a meaningful picture.

If you can, try to avoid setting up unrealistic expectations for your older child – and ask relatives and friends to do the same. In most cases the new baby won't be 'someone to play with' for at least another year or two, so telling him that he will be getting a playmate is misleading. If you are planning for friends or relatives to look after your other children when the new baby arrives, it can be helpful for them to know that it's common for small children, especially, to show more neediness when there are big changes in the household, and for their behaviour to become more babyish for a while. This doesn't usually last long (see page 70), provided the child feels his needs are accepted.

are an ideal time to think about how you would like to do things when your baby is new. The following questions may help you to start planning:

- Do we want to be in our own home or staying with relatives?

- Who do we want to visit and who would we prefer stayed away for a while?
- Is there anyone we would like to come and stay, to help look after us?
- What can we do to make meals and housework easy?
- What sort of help might we need to care for our other children?

'We waited 10 years for our first child, so we had lots of time to think about having children. We felt ready to put down everything else in our lives in order to pick this up. We didn't think of the kids as troublesome – they were just babies with babies' needs, and it was our job to deal with those needs.'

Joseph, father of John, 7, and Darragh, 2 years

What you need to be a 'good' parent (and what you don't)

The secret to being the best parent you can be for your baby is *you*. It isn't about equipment or gadgets, the latest educational toys or baby yoga – it's about the way you interact with your child every day. But the images of babies that we see in the media – in advertising, magazines, film and on TV – contribute enormously to our assumptions about what life is like with a baby and what being a good parent involves. Babies are pictured sleeping peacefully in a cot or playing with a mobile or baby gym, surrounded by toys and special furniture in a beautifully decorated nursery. Shops and websites that sell baby-care products have long lists of 'essentials' for parents-to-be. Given all of this it can be hard to avoid the idea that your baby must have certain things if she's to grow up safe and happy.

Many mothers and fathers find buying things for their baby is an important part of nest-building, and expectant parents are often given presents and hand-me-downs from friends or relatives. However, once their baby is born many find they don't really need all that much equipment. Some even say that a special room thermometer, for instance, can have the effect of making them distrust their common sense, while others find that some items can actually come between them and their baby and get in the way of their developing relationship. Babies need human interaction, and most prefer their parents' company to anything else. From a baby's perspective, toys and gadgets are likely to be a poor substitute for the movement and stimulation she gets when she is carried and talked to, or for the closeness of another human being. Of course, there are lots of things that may be useful or make life easier occasionally, but most won't be as meaningful for your baby as contact with you. She won't necessarily miss out if you decide you can get by without them.

'With my first baby I bought a baby bath thermometer and a special baby bath. It never occurred to me that she could just come in the bath with me.'

Jen, mother of Ella, 5 years, and Dorothy, 8 months

Becoming a parent can be exciting and daunting in equal measure. The key to finding your own way is to recognise the uniqueness of you and your baby, and to know that no one has trodden this path before. As far as being a parent to *your* baby is concerned, *you* are the trailblazer.

Key points

- Your expectations about parenting are likely to be informed by your own childhood, by what your peers do, by images in the media, and by the legacy of previous generations.

- It's impossible for babies to be 'good' (or not good), and a baby's behaviour is not a sign of good or bad parenting.
- Pregnancy can be a good time to begin to develop a bond with your baby, and for planning ahead for your first few hours, days and weeks with her.
- Much of what can seem like essential baby-care equipment isn't really necessary, and some may even get in the way of close and intuitive parenting. It's your loving presence your baby needs most.
- The reality of parenthood may be different from what you expect; be prepared to do things in the way that works best for you and your baby.

3

Welcoming your baby

The moment you meet your baby, and the time you spend with him immediately after the birth, is likely to be a profoundly moving experience. You will not only be welcoming him but helping him to adjust to what, for him, is a completely new existence, very different from anything he has known so far. For both parents these first hours can be intensely emotional and both have an important part to play in helping to make their baby's transition into the world as gentle as possible. From your baby's point of view, though, it's his mother who plays the central role. The physical connection he has with her means their experiences during this time are intimately linked, and they are each dependent on the other for their health and well-being. Understanding how this unique relationship works and why it matters is key for both parents, so that, together, you and your baby can make the most of this extraordinary time. However, for ease of understanding, 'you' (in this chapter) most often means the mother.

The need for closeness

Birth is enormously stressful for a baby. Having been squashed and squeezed, he is suddenly aware of cold air on his skin, of brightness in his eyes and loud, unmuffled sounds. He feels air in his lungs for the first time and finds he can move his limbs beyond the familiar restriction of the womb. For mothers, too, labour and birth are an overwhelming experience – mentally and emotionally as well as physically. Because of this, both mother and baby feel an intense, instinctive need to be close to one another in the minutes and hours that follow the birth.

This need for physical closeness makes sense. Just as when he was in the womb, from the moment a baby is born his mother is the ideal person to keep him warm, fed and protected. In those first precious minutes after birth, if he is laid against her chest or tummy, skin on skin, he can hear her voice and her heartbeat and feel the motion of her breathing, just as he could in the womb. Her skin will keep him warm, her movements will help to stimulate his breathing and her touch will calm him. This closeness lessens the shock of his arrival in the world; it helps him to adjust to the strangeness, and to feel safe.

Research shows that a period of uninterrupted skin-to-skin contact like this plays an enormously important role in

The physical benefits of skin contact

Skin-to-skin contact is physically as well as emotionally important for babies. Here's what happens when a baby's body is in direct contact with his mother's:

- His temperature is regulated – skin-to-skin contact is the most effective way of keeping a baby warm, and the chest of a new mother naturally warms her baby to the ideal temperature.
- His blood pressure is lowered and his heartbeat settles.
- His breathing slows and he gets more oxygen.
- Natural 'friendly' skin bacteria transfer from his mother's body to his, helping to protect him from infection.
- His digestion is stimulated, so his stomach is ready for his first feed.
- His growth and brain development are boosted.

helping both mother and baby recover from the birth. In the first minutes, while they are still connected to one another by the umbilical cord, the baby's touch against her skin will help the mother's womb to contract and push out the placenta (afterbirth). It will also help the baby's body to make the physical adjustments needed to survive outside her body.

A healthy, full-term baby is naturally in a state of quiet alertness in the first hour or so after birth, maximising his receptiveness to new experiences and learning (babies who are unwell or born early may not behave this way until later). His main task is survival and, as far as your baby is concerned, that depends on you, his mother. He needs to learn to recognise you by sight, touch and smell and to elicit your attention – to make sure that you recognise *him*. His eyes focus best at the distance between your breast and your face – everything else is a bit fuzzy – so having his head at the level of your breast gives him the best chance to see your face clearly. He is primed to gaze into your eyes, forging a connection that makes you want to protect and care for him, and respond to his needs.

Skin contact is what *you* are primed to expect, too. Focusing on your baby and allowing him to lead the way will awaken your instincts, so that you respond to him naturally, without needing to think about it. Most women the world over follow the same instinctive pattern of behaviour when they meet their newborn baby this way: feeling his skin, stroking him, counting his fingers and toes, inhaling his wonderful newborn smell and, prompted by his wide-open eyes and dilated pupils, returning his steady gaze.

'Zoe knew exactly what she wanted as soon as she came out – and that was *me*. And it was fine once I realised I was all she needed – because I needed her, too.'

Jane, mother of Zoe, 2 months

Having your baby's skin against yours will stimulate the release of two important hormones into your bloodstream. Prolactin, the mothering hormone, will trigger your drive to protect and nurture your baby and kick-start the production of breastmilk, while oxytocin, the hormone of love and labour, will 'open' your emotions, making you more trusting and responsive. Oxytocin will also dull your sensitivity to pain and to your environment, helping you to focus on your new baby. When he nuzzles your breast and begins to suckle, these two hormones will be released in huge bursts, making their effects even greater. Together they will help to put you both into a heightened state of awareness, enabling you to absorb information about one another easily and rapidly, and making the gradual process of attachment (or bonding) easier. Many mothers say they feel completely taken over by their baby during this intense time, and research shows that those who have had this experience are more likely to become attuned to their infant and find it easier, later, to understand his needs. Babies, too, show greater calmness and responsiveness when they have spent a prolonged period of time in skin contact with their mother at birth. By contrast, lack of touch at this important time can lead to raised stress levels in both mother and baby and a profound sense of 'not-rightness' that disappears as soon as they are together again.

'Ella needed to be checked over when she was first born. I saw her briefly and heard her cry, but I wasn't able to hold her till the midwives were happy she was okay. I felt a really strong need to touch her but I thought I was being irrational. When I eventually held her I felt like I didn't ever want to let go of her again. I didn't want anyone else to hold her. She was the only thing that mattered.'

Ruth, mother of Ella, 8 months

Skin-to-skin contact helps your transition to motherhood, as well as your baby's transition to his new life. The earlier it happens, the better; if it's not possible straight away, try to make it part of your first proper meeting with your baby (see page 50).

Skin-to-skin tips

There are no rules about how mothers and babies should behave at the moment of birth – letting your instincts and your baby lead is what matters, not whether you're doing it 'right'. However, there are a few things that are worth knowing, because they will help you to respond to one another easily. The most important is that skin-to-skin contact works best when it's exactly that – your baby's skin against yours, with nothing in between. That way your body can keep him warm, and both of you will be better able to tap into your instincts. Some mothers like their baby to have a nappy on but he shouldn't be wrapped or dressed. He will need to be dried quickly first, though, so that he doesn't get cold (unless you have a water birth – see below).

Most mothers find lying back against some pillows is comfortable for them, while also allowing their baby to move around easily. Leaning back like this will mean your baby can lie on his tummy on top of you, with as much of his body as possible touching yours, making it easy for him to lift his head and to see your face. A lightweight blanket or towel draped over his back will keep out any draughts and help to make him feel secure. If his hair is damp, a hat will stop him losing heat through his scalp as it dries.

If you have a water birth you may be able to stay in the water skin to skin with your baby for a while after the birth; some babies even have their first breastfeed in the pool. Keeping the water warm, and the level above your baby's shoulders, will help to stop him losing heat.

Unless you or your baby are ill, skin-to-skin contact can happen after a caesarean birth, too. Most obstetric surgeons and paediatricians are more than happy for babies born this way to be put straight on to their mother's chest (especially if they know in advance that this is what she wants). If it's not possible immediately, skin contact can usually start as soon as mother and baby are out of the operating theatre. You'll probably find you need your partner (or other helper) to help you to lie comfortably and hold your baby safely, especially if you've had a general anaesthetic. You may need to be creative in the way you hold him, so that he doesn't press on your wound, but as long as most of his body is touching you and he can get to your breast easily, his actual position doesn't really matter.

If your baby was born with the help of a vacuum pump (ventouse) or forceps, he may have bruising or a headache. Skin contact has a pain-relieving effect, so it is an ideal way to help him recover from such a traumatic arrival. However, he may be irritable for the first few hours and you may need to take extra care to avoid touching his head.

Skin contact with twins

Skin-to-skin contact is possible with twins, just as it is with single babies – although, if you have a vaginal birth, you may not have the opportunity for more than a quick cuddle with the baby who arrives first before handing him to your partner so that you can give birth to the second one. Once both babies are born, you'll probably need a little help to position them on your tummy, especially if you're on a narrow delivery bed, but that's really the only challenge – they will be used to sharing a cramped space and to touching each other, so the lack of room won't be a problem for them.

'Joe was put on top of me as soon as he was born and he crawled up to my breast by himself. He fed that way for the first couple of days – it was amazing. It was so different with Riley. I didn't really know about skin to skin then and I was all doped up and the hospital gown was on the wrong way round, so it was all a bit awkward. By the time I had Joe I knew what I wanted and how to ask for it – I had Joe snuggled on my chest all day.'

Nell, mother of Riley, 5 years, and Joe, 5 months

Your baby can lead the way

Almost all babies placed on their mother's tummy after birth follow a set of natural, instinctive behaviours aimed at helping them find their way to the breast. This is an important part of the adjustment to being born, and it's as relevant for mothers and babies who go on to bottle feed as it is for those who breastfeed. The sequence is the same for all babies, although each baby will progress through it at his own unique rate. Assuming your baby is well at birth, and not overly sleepy or premature, this is what you can expect him to do:

- He'll give a brief birth cry, then he'll relax against your body.
- He'll search out your face and gaze at you, examining you intently. He may turn his head towards your voice, which he'll recognise.
- He'll begin to 'crawl' towards your breast by pressing his feet into you and pushing himself along, using your natural scent as a guide.
- He'll move in short bursts, with occasional pauses for a rest.
- When he reaches your breast he'll start to bob his head around to find your nipple, then he'll begin nuzzling and licking.

- Eventually, he'll co-ordinate his movements sufficiently to tilt his head back, open his mouth wide and use his tongue to scoop up a large mouthful of breast. He may let go, wriggle around, and bob his head up and down several more times until he finds a 'latch' that feels right; then he'll start to suck.
- He'll feed rhythmically for a while and then he'll fall asleep.

This is something newborn babies instinctively do, and allowing your baby to work his way through the sequence at his own pace is an important part of helping him to recover from the birth and to begin to feel safe. He probably won't need you to help him, other than by supporting his weight so he doesn't fall sideways – he is on a mission and he knows what he's doing. Some of his pauses may be quite long and it may seem as though he's lost interest; he hasn't – he's more likely to be resting and absorbing all the new sensations. If you are woozy from drugs used during labour, or are particularly exhausted, you'll need to make sure your partner or someone else is there to support you and your baby, so that he will be safe if you fall asleep.

Some babies find their way to the breast and feed within the first hour. Many, though, are not very alert in the beginning, often because they have some of their mother's pain-relieving drugs in their bloodstream, making them drowsy, or because they are simply exhausted from a long labour or difficult birth. This can mean they take longer to move through the natural sequence of behaviours. Staff are sometimes tempted to put a baby who does not seem to be interested in breast-feeding into a cot, so that he can 'sleep it off', but this has been shown to interfere with babies' instinctive responses. Indeed, research has shown that newborns who are separated from their mothers before they have worked through the sequence described above have more difficulty learning to breastfeed effectively later. If possible, keep your baby with you, at least until he has found his way to your breast for the first time.

Although your baby is born expecting to breastfeed, his instinct to nuzzle at your breast isn't really about hunger – it's about learning to recognise you, feeling safe and starting to bond. For most mothers and babies, bonding takes place gradually, over the weeks following the birth (see page 55), but breastfeeding can help it to happen faster. It's a sort of shortcut, helping you and your baby to feel closer to each other sooner, and it can make the early weeks of parenting a bit less bumpy. Many mothers who didn't imagine they would breastfeed find themselves doing it almost by accident, just by allowing their baby to follow his instincts. Even if you have no plans to continue breastfeeding, letting your baby find his way to your breast at birth is a great way to begin your new relationship. If it isn't possible, try to make sure that his first feed – whether from your breast or by bottle – happens in what, for him, is a uniquely safe and familiar place – your arms.

'I was so emotionally dazed after the birth – it was so different to the one I'd imagined I couldn't quite work out what was going on. When Lilly was born all I could remember is that she had to go on to the breast straight away and I had to phone my mum. So that's what I did. I'd had so many drugs and was so exhausted from such a long labour I was delirious. I felt like I'd been hit by a truck for about four days!'

Sharon, mother of Lilly, 10 months

Staying together in the first hour or two

There's usually a lot going on in a busy labour ward, and staff are likely to want to check and weigh your baby fairly soon after the birth. However, many parents find it unsettling to have their initial contact with their baby interrupted, and the disruption can be confusing for babies too, especially if they haven't yet had their first feed. Indeed, babies whose instinctive sequence of movements is interrupted often have to start all over again. A skilled midwife can do most of the checks a newborn needs while he is lying on his mother – and having your baby to cuddle can be a good way to take your mind off being examined or stitched. Ideally, weighing him will be postponed until after he has fed, but realistically, if you give birth in hospital, your midwife is likely to need to complete the birth records as soon as possible – and he or she will need to know your baby's weight in order to do this. In this case, it may be better to have him weighed quickly, within a few minutes of the birth, rather than disrupting his instinctive responses to you. **It's reasonable for you or your partner to challenge anyone who suggests interrupting your skin-to-skin contact with your baby unnecessarily.**

Your partner's role in the first few hours

Your partner (or other birth companion) has a hugely important role to play in supporting you and your baby during this special time. Not only can they help you to get comfortable, and be ready with a towel or blanket to put over your baby's back and a cardigan or shawl for *you*, but their help can also be crucial in making sure that nobody disturbs you or separates you and your baby unnecessarily, and that your baby isn't rushed into feeding before he is ready. Your partner can also play a vital part in keeping other visitors at bay until you feel ready to see them.

'When I had my second child in hospital the midwife kept coming up to me, saying, "Oh, you're still doing skin-to-skin!" – as though you just do it for 20 minutes and then put the baby away. I remember a friend who had waited years for a baby – when I went to see her, the baby was in the cot. When I asked why, she said the midwife had put her there. It seems sad to feed your baby and then put her down instead of holding her, just because that's what everyone expects.'

Eva, mother of Ivan, 6 years, and Sofia, 15 months

If you have to be transferred to a different room or ward before your baby has fed, you can ask the staff to help you stay in skin contact with him during the move. If this isn't possible, aim to get back to it as soon as you're settled. If you can, avoid having a bath or shower until afterwards, so that you don't wash off the natural body scent that will help him find your breast.

'There were so many people around straight after the birth – it was all a bit overwhelming. I was so glad when we were finally on our own. We just spent ages staring at the baby and stroking her. She was just lying on me for ages – at least two or three hours. When my family turned up to visit I didn't have much on – I had Yasmin on my chest with a sheet over her. It was lovely they came, and they were desperate to see the baby – but it all felt a bit awkward really, and none of them got to hold her. It was too soon. We just needed to be on our own with our baby.'

Syeeda, mother of Yasmin, 5 months

The way you welcome your baby into the world can provide a springboard for the relationship you will develop with him over the coming weeks, months and years. Allowing yourself to be absorbed in the moment, as you get to know him in a gentle, unrushed atmosphere, will help you to be instinctively drawn in by his earliest expressions, sounds and movements, making following his lead later easier and more intuitive.

Skin-to-skin cuddles aren't just for newborns

Skin-to-skin contact doesn't have to be limited to the newborn period – cuddles like this are one of the easiest ways to calm and comfort a young child. Many parents find themselves instinctively wanting to touch their small child's skin when they are trying to soothe him, for example by putting their hand under his T-shirt so they can stroke his back. You can also warm your baby up this way if he is cold, or help to lower his temperature if he has a fever (see page 62). Skin-to-skin contact can also help to resolve some common breastfeeding problems – especially if you adopt the same lying-back position as you may have done immediately after the birth – because it enables you and your baby to go back to the beginning and start again.

What if I can't hold my baby straight away?

The optimum time to begin skin-to-skin contact is immediately after the birth, when your baby's instincts are at their strongest, but, if either of you is unwell or needs medical care, this special time may have to be postponed for a while. This isn't the end of the world – it just takes a little more effort if you've both got dressed in the meantime. Your baby may take a bit longer to begin to respond instinctively than if you had been able to hold him immediately, but, if you are patient and allow yourself to focus on him, he'll show you that he knows what to do.

If your baby is born very prematurely or is unwell at birth, he may need to be taken to the neonatal unit (NNU – also known as a special care baby unit, or SCBU) as soon as he is born. In that case skin-to-skin contact may have to wait until his condition is stable. Skin contact is enormously beneficial for premature and sick babies (see page 53), so make sure the staff know this is something you'd like to do.

'I had an emergency C-section with Jacob, and we were both trau-
matised for the first few days. All the time we were holding on to
each other it was fine, but as soon as we were separated he
would start crying – and so would I.'

Kelly, mother of Austin, 4, and Jacob, 2 years

Can dads do skin-to-skin?

The benefits of skin-to-skin contact are not confined to mothers and
babies. Men's chests, too, can provide warmth, calming movements
and soothing sounds, and research suggests that both mothers and
fathers who have early skin-to-skin contact with their baby become
more responsive and involved parents than those who don't. If for
any reason a mother can't hold her baby straight away, her partner's
chest is the next best thing – and far more welcoming for their baby
than a cot. However, if at all possible, in the first hour or two after
birth it's the bond between the mother and her baby that should take
priority. Pregnancy and labour have prepared them both for this
unique moment, which will never be repeated. This time is also
especially important for getting breastfeeding going, triggering milk
production and giving the baby the best chance to learn to feed
effectively from the very beginning.

Keeping your baby close while you're in hospital

If you have to spend the first days after your baby's birth in
hospital, aim to keep him as close to you as possible. Even
when he seems to be fast asleep, if you are holding him he
will still be aware of your smell, your heartbeat, your touch
and your movement. In previous generations, babies were
whisked off to the nursery, especially at night, so that the new

mother could rest. We now know that these early separations made it difficult for mothers and babies to get to know one another, as well as seriously undermining breastfeeding. In the long run, both you and your baby will benefit – and are likely to be more relaxed – if you stay close together.

'The second my hands left Daisy as I put her in the hospital cot, she'd cry. The minute I picked her up again, she'd be calm. It was instant. I asked the midwife what was wrong – she said, "She just needs a cuddle."'

Jenny, mother of Daisy, 6 months

Being close to your baby will also give you the opportunity to become familiar with the shape and feel of him and to learn the subtle signals he uses to show you what he likes and dislikes. For example, holding him with your hand on his back or chest will help you to get to know the rhythm of his breathing, how it changes as he feeds and sleeps, and if he is uncomfortable.

It's a good idea to make sure you can reach your baby easily without having to ask for help – especially if you have had a caesarean section or stitches and are finding moving difficult. The average hospital bed is likely to be too narrow to share safely with your baby but many hospitals have cots that attach to the mother's bed to make caring for the baby easier – you may want to ask whether a clip-on cot is available if you aren't given one routinely.

Staying close if your baby is in Special Care

If you and your baby have to be separated immediately or soon after the birth, your initial chance to get to know him may have to be postponed. By the time you are able to be with him, he may be in an incubator – perhaps connected to an assortment of tubes and wires to help him breathe, to feed him and to monitor him. All of this may well leave you feeling shocked, confused and powerless, especially if the birth itself didn't go the way you'd planned. Such a shaky start can make the prospect of holding and caring for your baby seem very remote and even a bit scary.

Although you may feel unable to fully share your baby's care in the highly specialised environment of a neonatal unit, it is enormously important that he has a sense of your presence, through your voice and your touch. Your voice and your heartbeat will already be familiar to him from the womb. He'll gradually begin to recognise your smell too (it may be a good idea to avoid wearing strong perfumes or scented toiletries, so that he can distinguish your own unique scent more easily). Even just putting your hand on his tummy will make a real connection between you, helping him to feel safe and loved. It will also contribute to his physical well-being, making his breathing more effective and helping him to grow. Your touch will be especially valuable if he has to undergo any uncomfortable or painful medical procedures, so he doesn't associate touch with discomfort. If there is a period during which he is unable to leave the incubator, spending time holding him gently, if possible with one hand cupping his head and the other cupping his bottom, will help him to feel contained and protected, like he did in the womb. Having a physical connection with your baby will help *you* to get to know *him*, too; many parents find this closeness enables them to recognise if their baby is becoming uncomfortable or stressed, so they can respond quickly.

Skin-to-skin contact is now known to be so important for premature and vulnerable babies that most neonatal units encourage a special version of it – known as **kangaroo care** – as soon as the baby's condition is stable. Kangaroo care is essentially an intense skin-to-skin cuddle. It mimics the way a mother kangaroo carries her tiny joey in her pouch and acknowledges the fact that babies born early still need to be in close contact with their mother's body. It's also enormously beneficial for breastfeeding. The staff will help you position your baby (in just a nappy) securely against your bare chest, probably with a stretchy wrap, so that he feels contained – just as he would if he were still in the womb. Holding him like this will allow you to have your arms free to stroke him (or hold a book or a drink) and, provided he is not connected to lots of monitors or other equipment, to move around.

Kangaroo care is great for babies and parents

Kangaroo care is hugely beneficial for premature or ill babies and their parents. Research has shown that babies who have frequent, prolonged periods of close contact with their mother:

- are less stressed
- have improved levels of oxygen in their blood
- have steadier breathing and heart rate
- maintain a more stable body temperature
- grow and gain weight better
- spend more time in restful sleep (thought to help with brain development)
- experience less pain
- are more likely to breastfeed
- are able to leave Special Care earlier

These effects are maintained way beyond the neonatal period: compared with other premature babies, those who have had this type of care have been shown to cry less and have longer periods of alertness for at least the first six months. Kangaroo care reduces maternal stress, too. And kangaroo care between fathers and babies encourages their bond as well. Overall, achieving this level of closeness helps both parents to feel connected to their baby, to understand his needs and to feel more confident caring for him.

The first time your premature baby is placed in your arms he may be startled by the new experience and push away from you. If he is attached to a monitor, his reaction may even set off an alarm. This is fairly common, and most parents find that staying as calm as they can themselves, and soothing their baby with gentle words or 'shushing' sounds, helps him to settle. The more time you spend close to your baby in the early weeks, the better you will get to know each other and the more quickly you will begin to feel confident about looking after him.

> 'Rudy came early but I held him skin to skin the day after he was born and put him next to my breast, even though he couldn't feed yet. I had him on my chest every day for about two hours and each time he was tube fed I'd put him to the breast. I think that association helped him a lot and helped me to produce milk. But even so, in the back of my mind I thought the incubator was the safest place for him. Now I wish I'd done much more kangaroo care.'
>
> Sophie, mother of Rudy, 15 months

Falling in love with your baby

There's a common misconception that parents, especially mothers, should fall in love with their baby at first sight and that, if they don't, they will have missed the chance to bond effectively. This can put them under unnecessary pressure to feel the 'right' way about their baby in the first few days or weeks. However, there is no time limit for bonding. Some parents feel they've been hit by a thunderbolt the moment they set eyes on their newborn or feel him in their arms, but most describe falling in love as something that happens over a period of weeks or months, as they get to know their baby.

Bonding means different things to different people. Some use the word to refer to the feelings of protectiveness or elation brought on by the emotional and physical experience of birth.

These feelings can be very sudden and intense, and quite over-whelming, but they are a long way from being the whole story as far as bonding is concerned. True bonding is the development of a deep, mutual attachment between parents and baby. It's some-thing that builds over time, as they get to know one another. For the baby, it's based on the growing sense of security and trust that comes from being held, talked to and cared for, and from having his needs and emotions acknowledged. For his parents, it may be a gradually increasing feeling of being in tune with their baby – something that grows alongside their confidence in caring for him, as newly learnt skills become second nature and they find themselves anticipating his needs and understanding his signals more easily.

Bonding can be different for each parent, and with subse-quent babies, as the quotes below show. Some parents can point to a specific moment, when their baby was a few weeks or months old, when they suddenly 'knew' he was theirs and that they loved him. Others say their bond continued to grow throughout their baby's childhood, with no obvious moment when they could have called it complete. For various reasons, including individual personality as well as external factors – such as a difficult pregnancy or birth, antenatal or postnatal depression, lack of support, or having to be separated from their baby at birth – some parents find that it takes longer than they expected to feel truly connected to their infant.

'I don't remember feeling a rush of love when Rory was born. It was more an overwhelming sense of responsibility. I focused on the practicalities first – all my thoughts were taken up with working out how to feed him and care for him. But it wasn't love exactly. Bonding just kind of happened over time. It was quicker with Jamie, maybe because I wasn't doped up after the birth and the physical discomfort afterwards didn't last as long. We had a lot more skin-to-skin from the start too – I was fierce about keeping him close and would've killed anyone if they'd tried to take him away. And I knew more about the practical side of looking after babies too, so I could focus more on him, as a person.'

Niamh, mother of Rory, 4, and Jamie, 1 year

'We waited a long time for Rory and I felt an instant bond. I remember seeing his face as he was born and lifted out. I utterly gave myself to him. It was very straightforward from the start. It was different with Jamie. It was a difficult birth so when he arrived I went into a practical, "let's manage this situation" mindset. I had more of a role this time, and it was functional rather than emotional. Until he was nine months Jamie had some health issues that meant he never really seemed comfortable; it felt like a barrier between us. Once he was better, he completely relaxed. One day he smiled at me and it was a different kind of smile – more complete somehow. That's really when I felt I bonded with him for the first time.'

Daniel, father of Rory, 4, and Jamie, 1 year

Bonding relies on close physical contact between parents and baby – you can't easily fall in love with someone you never get to see or touch. So if contact with your baby is delayed or limited in the beginning it may take you a little longer to experience a real feeling of love for him. It's not something that can be rushed but the more time you can spend holding him close, the more quickly your mutual attachment will develop.

Key points

- Skin-to-skin contact is the best way for a newborn baby and his mother to get to know one another. It's what both of you are primed to expect. It is just as important if the birth is complicated or if circumstances mean it has to be delayed.

- Babies are born expecting to breastfeed – and have the instincts that will help them to do it. They follow a natural sequence of behaviours that work best if allowed to unfold without disturbance.
- If possible, a baby's first feed, whether breast or bottle, should take place skin to skin with his mother.
- The main role of the baby's father (or other birth companion) is to support and protect the early closeness between mother and baby.
- Touch is vitally important for vulnerable babies. It comforts and soothes them, and allows bonding to start.
- Close, skin-to-skin contact with your premature or ill baby (known as kangaroo care) is an important way to enhance your relationship with him, and to promote his growth and well-being.
- Skin-to-skin contact is valuable throughout childhood as a way of promoting calmness and providing comfort.

4

The first few weeks

The first few weeks at home with their baby can be some of the hardest for new parents because the adjustment from their old life is so huge. Many describe it as a strange, dream-like time, where feelings of elation, exhaustion and anxiety at the responsibility of caring for a tiny baby can each be overwhelming in turn. Even when there are older children, the arrival of a new baby changes everyone's relationships. It can be a roller coaster of powerful emotions for the whole family. This chapter is about how to make the most of this special time as you get to know your baby, adapt to her rhythms and let her show you how to care for her.

Having a babymoon

The arrival of a new baby can be disorientating, even if this isn't your first child. The first two or three weeks are often particu-larly intense because they involve having to get to grips with feeding and the practicalities of baby care all at once, while still needing to get to know the newest member of the family. Some parents designate all or part of this early period as a 'babymoon', during which mother and baby can recover from the birth and both parents can negotiate their way through the array of new experiences and emotions with as few distractions as possible.

During a babymoon, the mother's relationship with the new baby is central. Her partner, wider family or friends take on shopping, cooking, housework and caring for older children, freeing her up to concentrate on getting to know her newborn, learning to recognise her needs and identifying her ways of communicating. It also allows her time and space to get to grips with breastfeeding.

> 'We really wanted a couple of weeks to get to know Amy – you never get that time again with your partner at home when you're not busy doing things. It's such a massive change for everyone and it's impossible to prepare for how you'll feel. It was lovely all of us being at home together.'
>
> *Sam, mother of George, 6, Eliza, 4 years, and Amy, 7 months*

Having a babymoon doesn't mean you have to shut yourselves away – unless you want to – but it gives you an excuse to keep less helpful visitors to a minimum (see page 68) and instead surround yourselves with people who will support you and with whom you really feel comfortable.

Your babymoon can last as long as you want it to but many parents find two weeks is a useful period to aim for. This allows a good start to breastfeeding and tends to fit well with parental leave. It's also likely to be a feasible amount of time to ask a close relative or friend to give up, to help look after you.

> 'Those first few weeks aren't that easy. You're still really uncomfortable from the birth and you're feeding all the time and trying to keep the baby happy and comfortable. The last thing I wanted when I had Lucy was someone I had to make tea for and entertain. I wanted to keep the noise around us down too. It's really hard to explain how protective you feel over a new baby. Some friends were okay – other mums maybe – but not anyone who'd want to hold the baby.'
>
> *Polly, mother of Oscar, 8, Martha, 4 years, and Lucy, 4 months*

A babymoon is traditional in many cultures

The idea of a period of privacy and seclusion with a newborn baby is becoming increasingly popular in the UK but it isn't new. In many countries around the world, new mothers are cherished and given time out from household tasks for up to 40 days, so they can concentrate on recovering from the birth and caring for their baby. In England, even as recently as midway through the 20th century, mothers were expected to have a 'lying-in' period of about two weeks to allow them to get their strength back. In mediaeval times this phase was marked by a piece of white linen, hung on the front door knocker to warn would-be visitors that they should come back another day.

Some traditional cultures consider the new mother to be unclean following the birth and give this as the reason why she is not to be involved in cooking, cleaning and caring for family members. Others place more emphasis on her need for quiet, in order to heal her body and produce good breastmilk. During this time she is cared for by other women from her family or community, who provide her with support and nourishment, for example with massages and special foods. In many societies the father is expected to visit only occasionally during this period, whereas in others he is seen as the mother's main supporter.

Why have a babymoon?

There are lots of benefits to having a babymoon. Many first-time parents value the chance it gives them to learn how to care for their baby without having to appear capable in front of others, or listen to (possibly conflicting) advice at a time when their confidence is rocky. The focus on closeness provided by a babymoon helps both mother and baby to relax and allow their natural rhythms and sleep cycles to become gradually synchronised (see page 147), deepening their connection and helping them to bond. Research suggests that mothers who keep their babies close to them and are themselves nurtured by a small group of caring relatives or friends may be less likely to suffer from postnatal depression.

Having a babymoon is an ideal way to get breastfeeding going smoothly. The first two weeks after birth are crucial for establishing milk production and getting to grips with the practical side of feeding, and a babymoon gives the opportunity for feeding to happen freely and often. If both baby and mother have the support they need to feed comfortably and effectively during this time, the chances of running into problems are vastly reduced.

The privacy and relaxation afforded by a babymoon means you can continue to enjoy skin-to-skin cuddles with your baby well beyond the first few days of her life, without being restricted by everyday routines or having to worry about who might turn up. It's not only a great way to make her feel safe and encourage bonding, it will also help regulate her temperature (see box, below) and make breastfeeding easier.

How skin contact regulates temperature

The best way to transfer heat from one body to another is skin to skin. Heat will always flow from the warmer body to the cooler one, so, if your baby's cold, just undress her and hold or carry her against your naked chest. If you wrap a blanket, cardigan, dressing gown or sling around both of you, she will be able to absorb warmth from your body without losing it to the surrounding air.

Skin contact can be used to cool your baby down, too. If she's feverish – perhaps because she is ill – then, in addition to giving her medication, if necessary, you can help reduce her temperature by holding her skin to skin. Don't be surprised if you start to feel hot – this is a sign that you are absorbing some of her excess heat, which your body is better able to deal with than hers.

'I don't have a partner so I stayed with my mum for the first few weeks after Amelia was born, and she looked after me. Amelia was in bed with me most of the time or right next to me – I really needed that quiet time to get to know her and to let her find her own way to breastfeed.'

Lisa, mother of Amelia, 7 months

Managing your babymoon

During the early weeks, a baby's primary relationship is with her mother. She relies on her mother's closeness to help make her transition from the womb as smooth as possible. It's a sort of 'wrapping-up' of the pregnancy, in which the mother and baby are adjusting to being separate. It's a time of intimacy and mutual observation – an intense period of learning and adjustment. Keeping your baby as close as possible during this time will help you to become attuned to her and allow you both to get to grips with feeding.

Making a mother and baby nest

Many mothers make a kind of nest for themselves and their baby during their babymoon. Your nest can be wherever you feel most comfortable spending lots of time feeding, dozing and snuggling. It could be in your bed or on the sofa, so you can feel closer to others in the house. (If you opt for the sofa or an armchair, you will need to take care not to fall asleep with your baby there, as this can be dangerous, see page 119.) Most babies prefer to lie in a curled position for the first few weeks, like they did in the womb, so persuading them to lie on their back in a cot can be difficult. Keeping your baby in your nest with you will allow her to uncurl gradually, in her own time.

Ideally, there'll be someone to look after you all the time, bringing you plenty of food and drink throughout the day. If you don't have anyone to keep you topped up, it may be a good idea to prepare a packed lunch, some snacks and something to drink whenever you get the chance, and to keep them nearby. You may want to have your phone handy, and maybe the TV remote control or a book, although many new mothers find they are too tired, on a baby-high or busy concentrating on feeding to get bored.

> 'The first few weeks were spent with me sitting on the sofa in my pyjamas with a couple of big cushions and Olivia feeding or sleeping. I was quite happy – I wasn't bothered about going out or seeing people. Neither of us could settle if we were too far apart – she just cried whenever she was away from me.'
>
> Nicole, *mother of Olivia, 11 months*

If you want or need to be moving around with your baby, carrying her in a sling will enable you to keep her close to your body, while leaving your hands and arms free so you can do other things. This is especially useful if you have older children to care for or if you don't have much support at home. Softer, wrap-style slings are generally recommended for newborns – see page 195 for tips on using a sling.

Giving yourself time to learn

Many new parents feel overwhelmed at the skills they are expected to master as soon as their baby is born. No matter how simple day-to-day baby care may appear from the outside – before you have a baby – the fragility of your newborn, and the fact that (like most babies) she dislikes being pulled about, combined with your own nervousness may well mean that something as basic as changing a nappy presents a major hurdle. Dressing and undressing can be particularly daunting – especially if you're still all fingers and thumbs. Some parents find keeping their baby in just a nappy, and holding her next to their skin (with a blanket or their clothes covering her back) so she stays warm, avoids the need to disturb her too much. Chapter 9 has some useful tips for making simple tasks enjoyable for both of you, but there's no need to rush – your baby really doesn't mind if her nappy's a bit skew-whiff or her babygrow is buttoned up wrongly. The most important thing to her is that you hold her, talk to her and provide her with food, warmth and love.

Where does Dad fit in?

The emphasis during the early weeks is likely to be on the baby's relationship with her mother, and it's not unusual for partners to feel slightly unsure of their new role. However, dads can be key to how smoothly the babymoon goes, making it easier for mother and baby to focus on each other. It's not just a case of taking on cooking, housework and the care of any siblings (or organising someone else to help with these things) – the father has a broader role of protecting the intimacy between mother and baby and supporting them emotionally, while also sharing the baby's care and beginning to establish his own relationship with her.

'Rowan changed our lives completely. It's like having a stick of dynamite under your priorities. The shape of our relationship changed, too. It *had* to, to respond to the new family we were. I was more than happy to be the support man – running around making tea, doing the shopping and cooking. It felt really important to do that in the early days so Noelle could spend the time feeding. It's the way we work things out anyway – if one has an area of expertise the other one gets out of the way and lets them lead the task. Noelle was definitely the expert when it came to the kids when they were tiny.'

Kieron, father of Rowan, 8, and Jack, 5 years

Although a young baby is likely to want to be close to her mother most of the time, especially if she is breastfeeding, spending time in skin-to-skin contact with her father will help to kick-start the process of bonding between them and allow his own nurturing feelings to flourish. She may enjoy being snuggled into his chest or neck, in his arms or in a sling, or sharing a bath with him (see page 189). This will help her to associate *his* smell and touch with feeling calm and comforted, too.

It's well known that women who spend a lot of time together influence each other's hormone levels, but research suggests that men, too, can undergo hormonal changes, both during their partner's pregnancy (if they are living together) and when the baby arrives. The chief effect is a rise in the hormones that trigger feelings of protectiveness (with an accompanying drop in testosterone). Many men are surprised to find how good they are at soothing a fretful baby and rocking them to sleep.

Many fathers take on the role of gatekeeper during the babymoon: answering the door and the phone, and making sure mother and baby are not overwhelmed with visitors. Some agree a secret sign or phrase that their partner can use to alert them when she's feeling fraught, so they can help steer a guest who has outstayed their welcome gently towards the door. Getting in supplies of food that won't need too much preparation, or stocking up the freezer with dishes that just need to be reheated, is another way fathers can help to make life easier and allow both parents to spend more time with their baby.

Don't be afraid to ask for help

You and your partner may well find you need some extra support during the first few weeks, especially if you have twins, or older children. Many new parents ask a family member or close friend to help out, although some opt to pay for a doula (somebody who specialises in providing practical and emotional support to families during the post-birth period, as well as in pregnancy and labour), or for someone to do the housework. Things are likely to run more smoothly if whoever is supporting you understands your need to discover how to be a parent and to find your own way with your baby.

'I spent a lot of time lying down with Ryan in the first weeks. I was so exhausted. Sean's mum came and cooked for us, and if she wasn't there Sean would be. A friend came and stayed for a few days and looked after me too – everyone was very good. We didn't have visitors as such though – just people looking after us. My first visitors were friends from work at six weeks. They took me out for a drink – it felt really odd.'

Miranda, mother of Ryan, 18 months

The first couple of weeks are when help at home is most useful, because this is when the baby's mother, at least, will be most exhausted and vulnerable, and when the baby needs her the most; but the longer there is help available, the better. If you do have someone else in the house, and your partner is entitled to two weeks' parental leave, he may want to consider taking the first week immediately and then the rest later, after the other supporter has gone, to extend the time someone will be around. Most parents find that having the support of others in their own home is more useful than going to stay with a relative or friend, partly because they may feel more comfortable there and partly because it allows their old life to merge into their new one more effectively.

Some partners find it particularly challenging to provide support when the mother is finding breastfeeding difficult or painful, because they feel there is little they can do to help. Understanding how breastfeeding works, and what is and is not helpful (see Chapter 6), can make a big difference. Sometimes the best way for a father to help may be to find out about local breastfeeding groups or make a call to a breast-feeding helpline (see page 229). Other times it may simply be a question of him showing his partner that he believes in her, and her ability to nourish their baby.

'Mothers need mothering so that they can look after the baby and cope with the challenges – because it *is* challenging. Having a child is one of the hardest things to navigate. It's hard without support.'

Sofia, *mother of Maxim, 6 years, and Anna, 14 months*

Managing visitors

Key to a stress-free babymoon is managing visitors so that you have the support that you need but the intimacy between you and your baby is not disrupted. Family and friends may be keen to see the new baby as soon as possible, but while some parents are ready for their baby to meet everyone straight away, others can feel their privacy is under threat.

Visitors, of course, vary. Some people will instinctively see their role as a supportive one and be enormously helpful. These are the visitors who arrive bearing food, or who roll up their sleeves and tackle a pile of ironing or the washing up. Others may simply be more interested in cuddling your baby. Most people will take their cue from you; if you don't particularly want your baby passed around for everyone to have a go, just keep hold of her. Your visitors will have to be content to stroke her head or have her grip their finger.

'Family and friends came to the flat just once in the first couple of weeks. I'd let others hold Alexandra but not for long. She seemed so vulnerable – I just thought it wasn't in her interests for other people to hold her. I think the grandparents worried that they wouldn't have any relationship with her if they didn't hold her when she was tiny, but it's not true – those relationships take time. She's very close to them now.'

Liz, *mother of Alexandra, 2 years*

If someone else *is* holding your baby, don't be surprised if you feel a bit twitchy, and anxious to have her back again. You may find yourself watching her extra closely, so that you can spot when she wants feeding, or when she has had enough and needs to be in your arms again. This is normal – and it's a sign that you are becoming tuned in to her needs.

'My gut reaction when Clara was born was to hold her close and not let go. I just didn't want to pass her round at all. If someone wanted to help, I'd say they could do the dishes, not hold the baby. One relative came wearing very strong perfume and held her – it was awful. When I got her back it felt as though that lovely newborn smell had been taken away. After that, I tried to be breastfeeding whenever anyone came, so they wouldn't ask to hold her.'

Julie, *mother of Clara, 10 months*

Studying new faces and trying to make sense of unfamiliar sounds and smells can be very tiring for a young baby. They need periods of quiet and the reassuring presence of a parent to help them process all this information. If they don't get it, they can end up overloaded and find it hard to calm down. It's not unusual for new parents to find that their baby is hungry, grumpy and unsettled after a day full of visitors, and that the evening and night are difficult as a result.

New parents sometimes find *they* are grumpy after visitors, too. Some feel too exhausted or emotional to deal with people; others find it stressful to try to soothe a fractious baby in front of others, when they haven't yet worked out the best way. The thought of breastfeeding in front of family and friends when mother and baby are still learning the ropes can also be daunting. For all these reasons, many parents find that working out who they want around them, and how long they want them to stay, can make a huge difference to how stressful (or not) they find the early weeks of parenting.

'My mother-in-law came round to help us every day in the first couple of weeks. She was great, she'd just be sweeping and washing up in the background, and if anyone came round she'd make them all tea. And she was really lovely with the baby, without taking over.'

Helen, mother of Alice, 8 months

Helping older children to adjust

With your first baby, the babymoon is all about you, your partner and your baby. When you already have older children they will be part of it, too. They need some time to get to know their new sibling, but they also need to adjust their relationship with you, especially if they have had your undivided attention until now. This is especially true of their relationship with their mother.

Children commonly regress to a more immature stage of development when they are struggling to cope with complex emotions, so you can expect your next oldest child, in particular, to be more needy as he undergoes this period of adjustment. He may look for repeated reassurance that you love both your babies and that you are not going to give him away or stop being his mummy or daddy just because you have a new one to care for. He may ask for extra cuddles or more attention at bedtime or during the night. If he was previously breastfed, he may ask to start again (there will be plenty of milk for two) – or he may just want to have a taste; if he is still breastfeeding, he may want to feed more often than usual. Many siblings say they hate the baby, or they want their parents to send it back. It's a difficult part of growing up, and the younger your older child is, the harder he is likely to find it – not only because he won't have the language to help him express and sort through his feelings but because this may well be the first time he has had to face anything this big.

The likelihood is that any step back into babyhood won't last long, especially if your child doesn't feel you are rejecting him. Hugs, reassurance and freedom to have a cuddle or breastfeed whenever he wants are likely to be more effective than being showered with presents 'from the baby'. While you'll often find yourself cuddling both children together, it may be a good idea occasionally to arrange for some one-on-one time with your older child. If you are sensitive to his signals and allow him to do what he needs to do to feel safe and confident, he will come to terms with the new situation in his own time.

You, too, need to adjust to being the parent of two (or more) 'babies' who will sometimes pull you in different directions. You may find yourself swinging between the needs of your new baby – to whom you are drawn because of her vulnerability – and those of your older child, and you may be surprised by the strength of these conflicting feelings. Meeting the needs of more than one child is, of course, something that will continue to present a challenge, but the immediate intensity of this period is likely to subside quite quickly.

'I loved us all being at home together. The main thing was to concentrate on the baby and make sure the other kids were happy. It was hard for Nick though. I wanted him to look after *me* but they thought he was there to play with them and take them out – they were so excited he was going to be home for two weeks.

But he's not used to them needing him so much and doing all the cooking for everyone. We probably needed more help in hindsight, but it's tricky – there wasn't really anyone else we wanted around.'
Sheena, mother of Louie, 6, Maya, 4 years, and Carmela, 9 months

Having a belated babymoon

It's never too late to have a babymoon. If the period immediately after your baby's birth was disrupted, for example by ill health or some other family crisis, having a belated babymoon can be a lovely way to mark the start of a new chapter. It's particularly valuable if your baby has had a long stay in hospital because of prematurity or illness.

Finally bringing your baby home from a neonatal unit is likely to be a big moment. It may also be nerve-wracking. Babies who are in hospital tend to be subjected to routines and schedules – either because their health requires it or simply because that's how hospitals work. In this case, however much you have been looking forward to having your baby home you may find it hard, at first, to trust her to tell you what she needs – and to trust yourself to provide it. A babymoon will allow you to get to know her on a deeper level than may have been possible so far. It will enable you to learn to respond to the subtlest of her signals in the way that feels most natural to you, without anyone watching. It's also a gentle way for her to get to know her new surroundings and to begin to forget the bright lights, loud voices and beeping machines that she has been used to until now.

A belated babymoon is really no different from one that takes place straight after the birth. If both parents can't be at home, see if you can persuade a friend or close relative to come and stay for a week or two, to give you moral and practical support during this special time.

'Reuben was born early. We came home just before his due date and made a real effort to go with what he needed. It's so routine-based in hospital – it's really hard to take responsibility and trust your own baby when you leave.'

Lyn, mother of Reuben, 13 months (born at 31 weeks)

Adapting to your baby's rhythms

Your baby is likely to spend most of her time in the first few weeks either sleeping or feeding, with short periods in between when she will be watching and listening to what's going on around her. Exactly *when* she wants to do these things, and for how long each time, may be quite unpredictable and make little sense to you at first, which may make life feel chaotic and out of control. Many babies are at their most wakeful in the early hours of the morning and, although this can be hard to cope with, it's perfectly normal (see page 134). Some babies seem to continue the pattern they had in the womb, perhaps sleeping a lot during the day and being more active at night, but even that is apt to change from day to day. All of this can make life exhausting for new parents.

'I really wanted some predictability in the early weeks. I thought a routine would make it better but everything took ages because she just wanted to be with me when she was supposed to be in the cot or having a bath or something. Eventually I realised the only way she'd be happy was if I went along with what she seemed to want. I had to be strict about responding to *her* – not the routine. It was easier after that.'

Molly, mother of Freddie, 4 months

Parenting is a 24/7, full-on experience; you may long for there to be a recognisable pattern, just so you know where you are. Some parents are drawn to the idea of a fixed routine, with set times for sleeping and feeding, but these tend to overlook the personality, unique needs and developmental stage of an individual baby – *and* the unique personalities and needs of her parents. New babies need time for their sleep patterns to adjust to day- and night-times (even people who promote sleep training generally agree that it shouldn't start until the baby is over six months old). Babies also need to feed frequently, and whenever they ask; schedules can be disastrous for breastfeeding. Many parents who have tried to schedule their baby's care find the effort outweighs any gain, simply because ignoring a crying baby, or trying to make her sleep when she doesn't want to, takes a lot of effort and is in itself exhausting.

Eventually, your baby will develop a pattern of her own that is closer to yours, based on her needs and your shared experience. In the meantime, it makes sense to throw away the clock, stay close to her, respond to her needs as they arise and take one day at a time.

'I wish I'd known in the early weeks that they don't stay like that forever. You basically just have to do whatever they need at the time. Because everything changes – and it really does get so much easier as they get bigger.'

Alison, *mother of Florence, 4 years, and Jessica, 7 months*

Key points

- The first two or three weeks as a new parent are particularly intense. A babymoon can give you a chance to adjust to your new role and get to know your baby. It's especially good for breastfeeding.
- Keeping your baby really close will help you anticipate her needs and begin to build a strong relationship.
- A babymoon gives lots of opportunity for extended skin-to-skin contact with your baby, which is good

for her general well-being, for breastfeeding and
for bonding.

- It can help to have someone to act as supporter and
  gatekeeper, enabling and protecting the intimacy
  between mother and baby.
- Choosing who you want around you in the first few
  weeks is an important part of nurturing yourselves and
  your baby.
- Older siblings may need lots of support to adapt to a
  new baby brother or sister.
- A belated babymoon is a great way to help you settle in
  as a family if the early weeks were disrupted.
- Listening to your baby and allowing her unique pattern
  to emerge is likely to be easier for all of you than trying
  to fit her into a set routine.

5

Communicating with your baby

In a close, baby-led relationship, parent and baby are almost constantly communicating with one another, through touch, movement, facial expression and sound. Your baby can tell you what he needs but it's only when you show him you want to understand that he knows he's been heard. Listening and responding to your baby is the first step in allowing him to influence what happens around him – in other words, to have some autonomy. Through your responsiveness, he will learn to trust that his efforts to communicate work – that he can make himself understood and that he can change things. Two-way communication with your baby is central to baby-led parenting.

This chapter explains how babies communicate with their parents, from smiles and laughter to frowns and crying, from newborn coos to babbling and, eventually, first words. It looks at how to recognise and interpret your baby's body language as well as the sounds he makes, and how to respond to him in a way that will help you to continue to understand one another as he grows.

Your baby wants to connect

The moment your baby is born he is ready to communicate with you. He is primed to do this as soon as possible, to ensure his survival. His initial gaze will prompt you to look into his eyes and trigger your urge to protect and nurture him; then he will start to respond to your expressions. Within 20 minutes of birth most babies can imitate someone poking their tongue out. By the time they are a few days old, if someone frowns, smiles or shows a surprised expression, they will try to mimic them. It may take a while for your baby to work out how to do it, but it's deliberate (newborns don't seem to copy reflexes such as coughs and sneezes). Within a week he'll be actively seeking out ways to engage with you, trying to make eye contact and using sounds to get your attention; by five or six weeks he'll be smiling at you, too.

Like most people, babies don't want to be talked at – they want to join in. They know the rudiments of turn-taking and can hold simple 'conversations' well before they learn to speak. Even as a newborn, your baby will stay still and pay attention

Why your baby needs to communicate

A young baby can do very little without the assistance of his parents, so he has to find ways to get them to help him. Until your baby can crawl, if you aren't holding him he can't come to you – he has to call you. If he is hungry, he can't get himself a snack; he has to ask you to provide him with the opportunity to feed. If something interesting is out of reach, it may as well be a mile away, because he can't get to it on his own; so he needs to signal to you that he wants it. If he is cold or lonely, he can't solve those problems by himself and he can't tell you exactly what he feels, only that something is making him unhappy. Even if you have no idea what your baby wants, acknowledging that he needs *something* and trying to make him feel better will help him to trust you and feel safe. This is the beginning of him realising that he can have an effect on things and that you are someone he can rely on to help him change things in his world.

to you when you talk to him, watching your face and listening intently. If you pause to show him that it's his turn, and give him time to work out a response, he'll reply – perhaps by copying your expression, by uttering a small sound or even by moving an arm or leg. Your willingness to 'listen', and to acknowledge what your baby has to say – even if it's just a blink, a wriggle or a sigh – is a key part of becoming attuned to him, and will help you to understand what he is trying to communicate to you.

True communication between you and your baby happens when he tells you how he feels and you let him know, by your actions and your words, that you've understood. This cue–response pattern will become more intuitive with time and is the foundation for a healthy parent–child relationship. This is the sort of conversation that parents have with their baby many times a day. For example, you may notice your baby's signals of tiredness and say: 'You're looking sleepy … do you need a nap?', while starting to rock him gently. Encouraging him to 'talk' to you in this way, through expression, gesture and sounds, and responding to him whenever he does, is at the heart of baby-led parenting. But it means you have to learn his language. The more quickly you can do this, the easier you will find it to get to know him and care for him.

'I find myself talking about the most ridiculous things to her – I'm so excited about showing her the world. I can't believe it. I'll be saying over and over, "Oh, is that a tree, Olivia, is it a tree?" "Are you hungry, little one, are you hungry?" And she'll stare back – it's as though she's hanging on my every word.'

Nichola, mother of Olivia, 5 months

Understanding your baby's language

Over the first few months, a great deal of what your baby is likely to need can be provided simply by holding him close to

A dummy can get in the way

Dummies are sometimes used to soothe babies but they can hamper their communication, especially if they're used a lot. Having a dummy in his mouth can make it harder for a baby to produce sounds and copy facial expressions. It can also make it more difficult for his parents to read the signs that he is uncomfortable or needs to feed, meaning that their response is delayed.

A dummy can also soothe a baby artificially, or make him sleep for longer than he should, so that he doesn't immediately register his need for attention and doesn't call for help until things are starting to get too much for him. This can lead to problems with feeding, in particular (see page 104). Prolonged dummy use can affect how babies learn to speak, too, as well as the shape of their jaws (and later the alignment of their teeth) as they grow. If you want your baby to have a dummy, try to keep it just for short periods, when he needs help to fall asleep or he can't be soothed any other way.

you, because that takes care of warmth, comfort and reassurance. But he'll also want to communicate other needs, such as if he is hungry, sleepy, or needs his nappy changing. He is born with a range of ways to let you know he needs something and he'll be willing to try them all out to find out which ones work best. Some of your baby's movements, gestures, expressions and sounds will be easy to spot, but others may be missed until you get to know them. Some of them will be unique to a particular need, but many will have more than one meaning. You'll probably recognise patterns and combinations of signals at first, gradually picking up clues earlier and earlier, so that you get the message before he starts to cry.

The secret to learning your baby's language is to use your eyes, ears and sense of touch to detect changes in his mood. He can't talk, so most of his language will be physical. He may show you what he likes – perhaps waving his hand towards something that interests him, feeding more enthusiastically from one breast than the other, or being more relaxed when held or carried in a certain way. Or he may show you what he doesn't like, perhaps by squirming, arching his back or turning away. If he is uncomfortable, or cold, he may simply wriggle slightly. As you start to notice these subtle signals, and link them to what's happening, you'll get a sense of what your baby likes, what upsets him and what soothes him. You may be surprised at how quickly you get to know his likes and dislikes and find yourself deftly removing him from a situation you know he doesn't enjoy *before* he starts complaining.

Having a babymoon (see Chapter 4) can help you to get a head start at working out the subtleties of your baby's cues, and continuing to keep him close as much as possible after that will allow you to respond to him in a relaxed way. This is especially important if he needs something for which a bit of notice might be helpful. For example, spotting his earliest signals that he wants to feed will give you plenty of time to put aside whatever you're doing, grab a drink and a snack and get settled somewhere comfortable. If you're formula feeding and you put the kettle on straight away, you should be able to have his feed ready before he's fully awake. The more time you and he spend close together, and the more open you are to picking up his subtle cues, the more synchronised and easy the way you communicate will become.

> 'I kept Chloe with me all the time, pretty much. Sometimes it was obvious what was wrong – usually it would be hunger. If she was tired, a feed would send her to sleep anyway. That was all she needed for ages really.'
>
> *Hayley, mother of Chloe, 14 months*

Many of your baby's signals will be unique to him, and only recognisable by you. It's not unusual for parents (especially mothers) to develop an intuitive sense of what their baby needs well before anyone else has noticed there's anything amiss. In fact, many apparently easy-going babies only exhibit the calmness they do because their parents are so finely attuned to their needs. But no matter how sensitive you may be to your baby's moods and signals, you won't be in perfect harmony with him all the time. It's a case of learning by trial and error. Babies change, and, as their needs become more varied, their cues become more complex. You won't always know what's wrong – but trying to make it right and in turn being open to his response will show your baby that you are listening.

> 'I remember being on the bus with Sofia when she was very little and she was upset and crying. I tried everything – she wouldn't feed, didn't seem tired, wasn't wet. I didn't have a clue and was obviously struggling. Eventually some old ladies on the bus said, "Take some clothes off her, love – she's too hot!" They were right – but it takes experience to understand the signs.'
>
> Catherine, mother of Sofia, 2 years

Recognising different signs

Some of the signs your baby uses could mean different things at different times, and it may take you a while to work out what to do. Others will be very specific to one particular need, and be more obvious. The way he tells you what he wants is also likely to change over time, as he becomes more adept at communicating and you get more intuitive at picking up his signals. For example, as a very young baby, he's likely to ask to feed as part of waking up by, for example, turning his head as if trying to find the breast (known as 'rooting'), wriggling, opening and closing his fists and his mouth, and bobbing his head around. If there is no response, he may begin to smack his lips, whimper or start sucking on his clothes or fists (see page 113). Once you know these signs, it's relatively easy to identify them fairly quickly. As your baby grows, he is likely to develop a short-cut version of these cues, which may be unique to him, such as patting your breast or making a particular little sound.

> 'It was all trial and error with Josh, when he was little. I never knew what he wanted so I'd always try the breast first. If he didn't want that then I'd check his nappy or whatever. But usually if he started to wriggle a bit he'd want to feed.'
>
> *Melanie, mother of Josh, 9 months*

Recognising the signs that indicate that a baby is tired or feeling overwhelmed by too much stimulation is not always easy. Starting to cry or throw things is an obvious indication that an older baby has had enough of a particular activity, but the early signs (see box, overleaf) may be a lot more subtle than this, especially in the first few months. To a very young baby, everything is new, so he can quickly become overloaded just while watching someone's face or looking at a toy. A constant stream of chatter has a similar effect. Babies deal with this by temporarily switching off, perhaps by looking away or closing their eyes for a few moments. This allows them to absorb what they have experienced and file it away, so they can start a new page. If the signs of overstimulation haven't been noticed, efforts to re-engage the baby – for example, turning him so he has to make eye contact, talking animatedly to him, or shaking a toy in front of him – can quickly lead to exhaustion, frustration and crying.

Overstimulation can look very like tiredness, with signs such as grumpiness, rubbing eyes or pulling ears common to both. The clue to working out what's wrong is whether or not your baby is also showing signs that sleep is what he needs, for example, yawning, slowing down, and glazing over (see page 138).

Signs of overstimulation and tiredness

Here are some of the common signs that a baby is reaching the end of his ability to deal with a situation; your baby may display any or all of these – or develop his own:

- Pulling his ears
- Rubbing his eyes
- Fidgeting
- Hiccoughing
- Arching his back
- Turning his head or body away
- Sucking his fists or clothes
- Possetting (bringing up a bit of milk)

If you notice these signs, your baby probably needs some time away from whatever is going on. If he doesn't seem to want to go back to it, maybe the answer is to help him settle for a nap, if he is sleepy, or to let him have some quiet time with you, a change of scene or some fresh air. Be ready to rescue him from well-meaning friends and relatives who aren't able to interpret the signals that tell you he needs a break.

Other signs, such as wriggling, waving his arms, or being generally fidgety or grumpy may mean your baby is uncomfortable in some way. Perhaps he's wearing something that is irritating him (see page 192), or is feeling too hot or cold. If he's strapped into a buggy, he may need you to hold him, instead, or to be able to move about more freely. An older baby may simply be bored and in need of a change of scenery or a new game. Sometimes just picking your baby up and talking to him will be enough; at other times some detective work may be needed to figure out what's bothering him and how to make it better.

Signing with your baby

Babies readily understand gestures. This, coupled with their keen-ness to copy others, and their growing dexterity, means they can be helped to sign as a way of communicating, well before they are able to say the same things in words. Many parents use gestures with their baby as a natural accompaniment to talking, repeatedly using the same movement in a similar context. Babies eventually start to reproduce these gestures appropriately; for example, by about eight months your baby may spontaneously wave goodbye when someone is leaving. He may also come up with his own signs, such as lifting his arms when he wants to be picked up or carried. If you can work out what your baby means by a particular gesture, you can encourage him to use it, and respond appropriately each time he does. Even if it's not possible to give him whatever he's asking for, the fact that you acknowledge his attempts to communicate by showing him you've understood will boost his confidence and encourage him to expand his repertoire.

Baby signing is a more formalised extension of this natural use of gestures, and involves a set of agreed signs for numerous every-day things that babies may want to communicate, before they can manage words. The parent uses the sign while saying the word and, with repetition, the baby learns to associate the two. The most widely used signs include those for 'milk', 'all gone', 'hungry' and 'thirsty', along with signs for animals, cars, toys and so on. Signing can help prevent the frustration that many parents and their babies encounter, by giving the baby an easy way to show what he wants.

'Now Josie's bigger it's so much easier to know what she wants. Sometimes she just makes it clear she wants to be on my hip, and then she bounces around and waves her arms until I start walking. Quite often she just wants to be in a different room; other times she won't settle until I've taken her on a tour of the house! I think she just gets fed up of being in the same place after a while.'

Andrea, mother of Josie, 9 months

There'll probably be an element of guesswork involved in deciphering what your baby is trying to tell you – and maybe some frustration on his part – for several years, especially when what's troubling him isn't an everyday need. But communication between you will get easier and easier as your relationship grows and deepens.

Talking with your baby

Babies start to understand words long before they are able to use them. Research shows that by the time they are born they have already absorbed the rhythm and sounds of the language spoken by their mother, and can distinguish it from other languages. And by around halfway through their first year, most babies appear to recognise and understand common phrases and the names of familiar objects and people.

The way that adults – and even children – talk to babies is different from the way they speak to one another. Pretty much the world over, people use a softer, more sing-song, exaggerated type of speech with babies and their voice takes on a higher pitch. They often repeat phrases, too. This musical way of talking is sometimes called motherese or parentese, and it's thought babies are more responsive to it than to our ordinary speech. Most people exaggerate their expressions when they talk to babies, too, opening their eyes wider, smiling more and generally making their emotions more obvious than when they're talking to another adult. When you talk to your baby, you'll probably find yourself doing this intuitively.

As you talk, your baby isn't just listening to your stream of words; he is also noticing how fast you talk, the length and rhythm of your sentences, your overall tone, the rise and fall of your voice and your facial expressions. From this, he gets a sense of individual words and their meaning, and can also detect your mood. It helps him learn how to speak *and* how to recognise and understand emotion. Talking to him about *his* moods, using phrases and a voice and expression that match what you're saying (for example, 'You look happy – you're smiling!' or 'Oh dear, are you sad?') will help him to differentiate his own feelings, encourage him to communicate them and show him he can trust you to understand how he feels. Having you reflect his feelings this way (sometimes known as mind-mindedness) will also help him gradually develop an awareness of how other people feel.

Some parents feel self-conscious or unsure about talking with their baby. If you're struggling to know what to talk about, remember that it's giving your baby your attention – and allowing him to respond – that's the most important bit. Apart from picking up and commenting on his feelings, an

Your baby wants a proper chat

Babies and children want our attention when they're talking to us. Many parents find that their baby protests loudly or appears bewildered if he is interrupted in the middle of a 'conversation' – for example, when somebody engages with him, maybe by saying hello and playing a little, and then suddenly turns away or disappears out of sight before he's had a chance to respond. Lots of background noise can also be distracting or confusing. Just like adults, babies want to be able to focus on what the other person is saying – and, just as we do, they are likely to feel frustrated if other people and noises are getting in the way, or disgruntled if they are suddenly cut short. Whenever possible, give your baby the best chance of focusing on his conversation with you and the opportunity to have his say.

easy way to start is simply to talk about what's happening as you go through the day – for example, telling him what you're doing while you're changing his nappy, and asking him for his help. Babies learn to understand whole phrases very early, and if the same words appear in different sentences, they begin to recognise them out of context, too. So hearing: 'Can you just lift your leg for me?', 'I'm just putting your leg down now,' and 'See if you can push your leg out straight,' will help him to pick out the word 'leg' and understand its significance long before he is ready to say his first word. When you're out for a walk there'll be lots to comment on (dogs, cars, people, the wind, the sun, shouts and barks), but even the most mundane day at home can be made interesting: 'Oh look, here's the postlady! She's got a bright red shirt on today. She's bringing us a letter.' You don't need to invent baby words; repetition of simple words like 'shirt' will help to make them memorable, while incorporating them into sentences will show your baby how words work.

> 'I talk to Rose when I'm doing things with her – it's a bit like being a sports commentator but slower. I always make sure she knows what's going on and what's going to happen next, then I wait for her to respond, but I have to be patient. I'm sure talking to her like this has made her more relaxed. And she seemed to understand loads of words really early.'
>
> Caitlin, *mother of Rose, 11 months*

Getting ready for words

Your baby is getting ready to use words as soon as he begins to make noises to express meaning. He'll start by cooing, which will gradually turn into longer, more tuneful vowel sounds as he grows. From around five months, sounds such as 'Guh' and 'Buh' will herald the beginning of what's known as babbling. Towards the end of their first year, many babies are beginning to produce strings of sing-song babble as an accompaniment to their play, and some may even have one or two clear words, such as (the ones you've been looking forward to hearing!) 'Mumma' or 'Dadda'.

> 'When she's in the buggy, facing me, we talk much more. Sometimes she likes to face the other way but I don't hear her if she's trying to get my attention. Facing me gives her the opportunity to babble away to me if she wants to, and for me to join in.'
>
> *Sabina, mother of Georgia, 6 months*

What crying means – and how to deal with it

All babies cry sometimes but there's no need to wait until your baby cries before you respond to him. In fact, the sooner you can pick up on what he needs, the more quickly you'll be able to provide it and the more peaceful life will be. Young babies' cries sound heart-rendingly urgent – for good reason: in evolutionary terms their survival depends on immediate adult attention. However, most babies try to let their parents know they need something by a series of signals before they start to cry. If they don't get a response at their first attempt, they'll try something else, and if that doesn't work then they'll probably move on to crying. How quickly this happens depends on each baby's individual temperament and the urgency of the need at that time.

If you miss your baby's earliest cues, it's likely that he'll become more agitated in stages. For example, increasing wriggling, grunting, head-turning, kicking and whimpering are all signs that he needs you urgently and that crying may be about to happen. Once he does start crying, if there's no response the crying will become more insistent as he becomes increasingly frustrated and overwhelmed. The sooner you can let him know you are there, the better – not only because he will be easier to soothe but also because some babies, when they learn that crying is the only thing that works, start to skip the preliminaries and cry more readily. If it turns out that a cuddle is all your baby wanted, that doesn't make it any less important – when he is too young to understand time and place, a cuddle is the only way he knows he is safe and loved.

Your baby is more likely to get to the crying stage before you're able to respond if:

- you're not near enough to him to pick up his early requests for help (or you are distracted by something else)
- his need is sudden and urgent
- his need is something that hasn't cropped up much before, so you haven't learnt to recognise the signals yet
- his need is not something you can easily sort out (for example, he may be ill or in pain)

'I don't want to do anything that makes my children cry – it's just not me. With Beth, I've worked out the difference between a grumbling cry and proper upset – but I try to stop the grumbling as soon as I can because otherwise it quickly turns to upset.'

Joanna, mother of Elise, 4 years, and Beth, 3 months

Sometimes crying happens without any warning. Babies tend to cry as a first response to something sudden or unexpected – perhaps a bright light, loud noise or sudden movement. And they can start crying abruptly if they have been involved in play and haven't noticed that they are getting tired or hungry; by the time they realise something's wrong, the problem is already overwhelming.

Colicky crying

Babies who cry a lot, especially in the evenings, are often said to have colic. This regular, inconsolable crying can be extremely difficult for parents to cope with. It used to be assumed that colic was caused by a digestive problem, because the crying baby draws his knees up, as if in pain. However, we now know this isn't necessarily the case – babies frequently pull up their knees in an effort to curl themselves into a ball, just because they are miserable.

The reasons for colicky symptoms are not clear. Some breastfed babies who cry frequently (and have gassy poo) are in fact not feeding effectively; their symptoms often improve when they and their mothers are given help with their feeding technique. Rarely, babies who cry shortly after feeds throughout the day are discovered to have gastro-oesophageal reflux disease (GORD or GERD), in which the lining of their oesophagus is damaged; for them, medication may resolve the problem. However, for the vast majority of babies who are thought to have colic, the cause of the crying remains unknown and medication has little or no effect.

This type of crying usually gets better spontaneously by about four months; meanwhile, making sure your baby is effectively attached when he's breastfeeding, cuddling him in an upright position after feeding, carrying him in a sling or holding him upright for at least some of the day may help with colicky symptoms.

'Joe just needed to be upright the whole time – if I tried to put him in any other position he'd just cry. So he lived in the sling for the first three months – it was the only way I could do anything.'

Rochelle, mother of Joe, 11 months

For many babies, crying happens most often in the first few months, peaking at around two months of age, after which it begins to lessen. It's not clear whether this is because the baby is happier – because his early problems have resolved themselves – or simply because he has got better at communicating his needs (and his parents have become more skilled at meeting them). Either way, things tend to get better, not worse.

Babies' varying needs

Babies differ enormously in their tolerance for minor discomfort, in how quickly their needs become urgent and in how easily they can be soothed when they are upset. Some seem to be naturally more needy than others and parenting them can be very demanding. On the other hand, babies who don't ask for much attention sometimes end up not getting *enough*. If your relationship with your baby fits either of these patterns, you may find that building a strong bond between you needs to be a conscious effort (maybe through having plenty of quiet time together), rather than something that just happens. If your baby is very needy you may both benefit from some time apart occasionally, so that you can recharge your batteries, both emotionally and physically. This is where relatives and friends can help enormously.

Research suggests that babies are more likely to be needy if their mother was under stress for much of her pregnancy. It's thought the raised levels of stress hormones in a pregnant woman's system can affect her baby, causing him to be on high alert for much of the time, with a tendency to maintain this once he is born. Some research suggests that babies who are born prematurely are also inclined to be more irritable, as are babies who experienced a difficult birth. Babies are also sensitive to the emotional atmosphere around them – tension in the air can make them more prone to crying. But person-

Crying and birth trauma

Babies who have had a difficult or prolonged labour and birth, or who were delivered using ventouse suction or forceps, often have a headache for a few days, which causes them to cry. In some cases the problem lasts for several weeks. Obvious bruising can make it uncomfortable for the baby to lie or be held in certain positions and many prefer to be in an upright sling, so there's no pressure on their head. Where the cause of the pain is not obvious, or where the problem continues after any external bruising has disappeared, some parents find that treatment by a specially trained cranial osteopath or chiropractor can provide an answer.

ality plays a part, too; parents of multiples are often struck by just how different each baby's needs are.

'If my daughter was crying she would usually settle as soon as I held her, so I thought the same would work for the boys. If they were both crying I'd hold them both and try to soothe them. I could tell Daniel wanted me close – he would fall asleep really soon – but Joshua wouldn't calm down until I'd put him in his bouncy chair or the cot. It took me a while to work out that he needed his own space. I couldn't believe it – I thought a cuddle always worked. He's still like that now – much less cuddly than his brother.'

Nicky, mother of Chloe, 5 years, and Daniel and Joshua, 16 months

Whatever their general level of neediness, most babies go through phases of needing more attention and comfort than at other times, although the reason isn't always clear until afterwards, if at all. For example, many will have a period of being less resilient and more frustrated than usual just before they achieve a new milestone of development. It's not uncommon to find that a week or so of wanting to be cuddled very frequently is followed by the appearance of a new skill, such as rolling over or reaching out for toys. These episodes are often referred to as 'development spurts'. They're not fully understood, but knowing about them can help to solve the mystery of the occasional bout of unexplained neediness.

Ways to soothe your baby

However attuned you are to your baby's needs, there will be times when you are unable to stop him crying, and when you can't work out what's wrong. However, you won't always need to know exactly what the problem is to make him feel better; focusing on helping him to be calm and to feel safe and loved, rather than on stopping the crying, may work just as well.

Although crying in babies is usually triggered by stress, it can also be a way for a baby to 'let it all out', as part of dealing with complex emotions or overstimulation. This is one reason why babies don't always stop crying the instant the cause of their distress is removed; instead, once they feel safe (usually in someone's arms), they relax and settle gradually, as the crying releases the tension that has built up.

There are lots of ways to soothe babies who are upset. Different babies will respond to different things, and what works for your baby one day may need to change the next. Many measures help to alleviate physical discomfort as well as fulfilling a simple need for calming, so they are worth trying, even if you don't know exactly what the problem is. Top of the list, if you're breastfeeding, is to offer your baby the chance to feed. This will often do the trick, since it provides comfort, food, drink, warmth and your attention, all in one. (Formula feeding can't be used in quite the same way because of the risk of overfeeding, but a small feed may be helpful.)

Touch is a hugely powerful way to reduce tension and distress. Many parents intuitively combine touch with sound and movement – for example, holding their baby close while swaying rhythmically and making gentle, repetitive, sounds. You and your baby will almost certainly discover a few techniques of your own, but here is a selection of tried-and-trusted soothing suggestions to help you get started:

- Feeding – especially breastfeeding
- Sucking for a while on a (clean) finger, or possibly a dummy (but see page 80)
- Being carried or worn in a sling, or cradled in your arms as you walk, dance or sway
- Being held face to face, with you mirroring his gestures and expressions sympathetically, and talking to him in a soothing voice about how he is feeling
- Skin-to-skin cuddles, with a warm blanket round both of you
- Being held upright, nuzzled into your shoulder
- Being held tummy-down, draped along your forearm, in what is sometimes known as 'tiger in the tree' position (with his head towards your elbow, facing outwards; his arms and legs either side of your arm; and your hand cradling his crotch)
- Being laid, tummy-down, across your knee, perhaps with a gentle, repetitive movement produced by you flexing your foot
- Up-and-down rocking
- Rhythmic stroking or patting, or a gentle massage
- Lullabies and other songs and music (something with a steady beat is good)
- Gentle background noise or white noise, for example low, even talking or 'shhh' sounds, taped 'womb music' or the sound of a vacuum cleaner or tumble dryer
- Sharing a warm bath with you
- A trip in the car, buggy or sling
- A change of location – going home, into the fresh air,

into a quiet, dimly lit room or just away from
overwhelming stimuli

It's easier to respond effectively to a crying baby if you give
him your full attention. If your mind is elsewhere you are
less likely to pick up the cues that will tell you what the
problem is, and whether what you are doing is helping.
Attempts at distraction, for example, with a toy or something interesting, may be helpful for an older baby but are
unlikely to work with a very young baby, or one who is
seriously distressed. From his perspective, he may already be
overloaded with sensations and feelings that he can't move

Your baby can sense your mood

For the first few months, a baby isn't aware that he is a separate
person from his mother (and then only very dimly). When she
holds him or talks to him, he immediately senses her feelings and
may start to feel them for himself. So, if you are feeling anxious,
your baby may become anxious, too. This can make coping when
he's unsettled very difficult, because if he's crying furiously and
nothing seems to work, it's very likely you'll find your own stress
levels rising.

Some parents find that simply handing their baby to someone
else (and taking a break) when they begin to feel stressed is enough
to calm both them and their baby. Others find they need to concentrate on releasing tension, perhaps using deep breathing, music or
yoga, or taking a bath, going for a run or chatting to a supportive
friend. Being on your own in the house with a screaming baby can
make everything seem worse than it is, and make relaxation impossible. Lots of babies calm down in the sling or buggy when they are
outside, and simply getting out of the house can help an over-
stressed parent too, just by giving them a change of scene.

---

past; he's likely to need help to manage his emotions and regain a feeling of calm before he will be able to devote his attention to anything else.

Sometimes the cause of the problem will suddenly become clear while you're focusing on soothing your baby; at others, whatever triggered his crying will sort itself out spontaneously, or you'll fix it without even realising. Either way, just holding him and talking to him gently is likely to play a huge part in helping him to recover and feel happy again.

'Millie was always much happier when we went out to baby groups. I think it was because I was more relaxed, chatting to other people. When I was at home I'd spend all day on my own worrying about what was wrong with her and wondering why she wasn't doing what the book said. I'm sure she picked up on it and it made her anxious, so she'd be really unsettled.'

Lauren, *mother of Millie, 8 months*

The fact that your baby cries occasionally (or even a lot) doesn't mean you are not doing well as a parent – it's not crying itself but *unanswered* crying that is thought to be difficult for babies to overcome. What's important is that you recognise that he's distressed and respond to him sensitively, even if you can't immediately work out what he needs. That way he will feel valued, loved and safe, and his trust in you will be reinforced.

'Every now and then Daisy goes through a difficult time, when she's really grumpy, can't settle and just wants to be close to me all the time – it can be exhausting. I've learnt that if you just go with it and try to be sympathetic, whatever the problem is, it's resolved much quicker. If you fight it, it takes much longer for them to work through it.'

Katy, *mother of Eliza, 6 years, and Daisy, 9 months*

Talking to your baby, listening to him, learning his language, and discovering how to respond to him sensitively are all skills you'll continue to fine-tune as he grows, at the same time as he is developing his own communication skills. Letting him lead the way will foster a deeper understanding between you, minimising the chances of frustration and conflict and making parenting easier and more rewarding.

Key points

- Babies are born expecting to have 'conversations' with other people, to be listened to and to find ways to ask for what they need.
- Babies communicate with their body, their face and their voice. To communicate effectively with your baby you need to learn to understand his language.
- Dummies can make communicating and learning to talk more difficult for babies.
- Your baby doesn't mind what you talk to him about – as long as you talk to him.
- There's no need to wait until your baby cries before you respond to him. Being tuned in to his subtle ways of communicating his needs will make life easier all round.
- All babies have different needs, and your baby's needs will vary, both from day to day and as he gets older. The more flexible you are, the easier you'll find it to adapt.
- Some crying is inevitable. It's responding to it that matters, even if the problem that caused it can't be solved.
- Babies can quickly become overwhelmed by powerful emotions, which makes it more difficult for them to communicate what's wrong.
- There are lots of ways to soothe babies; you may have to try out a few before you find what works for your baby.

6

Baby-led feeding

Feeding is a key part of the parent–baby relationship. In the early months it's a special, intimate way for you and your baby to get to know each other – an opportunity for cuddling, closeness and communication. And, as she moves on to solid foods, it will evolve naturally into a shared family and social activity. Giving your baby the opportunity to eat is central to your role as a parent but, from the first breastfeed to when solid foods eventually take over, babies know what they need and when, and they know how to feed themselves (although they need a bit of practice at first). Allowing your baby to be your guide is the secret to an easy, loving and nurturing feeding relationship.

This chapter explains why being baby-led is so important to feeding, and how to allow your baby to take the lead from the beginning. Much of it relates to breastfeeding, since this is the way all human babies would feed if we followed a biological course, but, as you'll see, there are lots of ways to make bottle feeding baby-led, too. The final sections are about how your baby can join in with family mealtimes, discovering solid foods for herself as she embarks on baby-led weaning.

Baby-led feeding makes sense from birth

All healthy babies have the ability and the instincts to play an active role in making sure they are well nourished, from the moment they are born. For instance, they know *when* they need to feed. They are acutely tuned in to their hunger and thirst levels and are able to ask for what they need, when they need it. They can also be trusted to know *how much* food they need. Your baby's needs will vary from day to day, just as yours do, but as long as she is healthy (and, in the early days, not too sleepy, see page 114), she can judge her own appetite.

Baby-led feeding means:

- recognising the signals that tell you your baby wants to feed
- allowing her to feed whenever she wants
- allowing her to choose how fast she feeds
- allowing her to decide when to finish feeding

A baby's instinct for survival is very strong. Because of this babies *expect* to lead the way when it comes to feeding. **Trusting your baby to know when to feed and how much milk to take is the essence of baby-led feeding.**

However, feeding isn't only about hunger – it's also about comfort and closeness. Babies ask to feed because they're hungry, thirsty, frightened, too cold, too hot, lonely or ready to sleep. If your baby is breastfed, all of these needs can be met at the breast with no risk of overfeeding, because, provided she is given the opportunity to feed whenever she asks, a breastfed baby will regulate the pace herself, to make sure she doesn't take more milk than she needs.

You can let your baby take the lead if you are bottle feeding, too, but because she won't be able to control the feed in the same way, you may need to be a bit more shrewd about interpreting her signals, so you don't end up giving her milk when what she really wants is a cuddle.

Feeding is naturally baby-led

For a newborn baby, a key part of feeling safe is being near her mother's breast. She expects to breastfeed soon after she's born – even though she isn't hungry yet. She doesn't need to be taught how to do it, or have anyone put the nipple into her mouth for her – she just expects the breast to be there, so she can help herself. Allowing your baby to lead the way with her first feed, in her own time (see page 45), can make a huge difference to how easy you both find breastfeeding long term. And because breastmilk is always available 'on tap', it's easy to keep feeding baby-led from then on.

Being baby-led is also by far the most effective approach when it comes to breastfeeding because a mother's breast-milk production relies on her baby 'putting in her order' (see page 104). Allowing your baby to feed whenever she wants, as fast as she wants and for as long as she wants means your supply will match her needs and keep pace with her growth. It will also help you to avoid problems such as engorgement (painfully overfull breasts) and mastitis (an area of soreness and inflammation in one breast), which can sometimes be the result of restricted feeding.

'Breastfeeding is like a big, massive hug. You spend so much time hugging each other there is no way you are not going to bond. I'm sure it made everything easier for us.'

Miriam, mother of Nathan, 6 years, and Annabelle, 10 months

Bottle feeding can be baby-led, too

A baby feeding at the breast naturally sets the pace herself – in fact it's pretty much impossible to hurry her or to make her feed when she doesn't want to. And, because the milk changes in consistency and the flow tends to slow towards the end of the feed, she is able to tailor the feed to match her appetite.

However, when a baby is fed by bottle – whether with formula or expressed breastmilk – the consistency and rate of flow are more or less constant, so it's easy for her to take more milk than she really needs. This means parent and baby need to manage the feed *together*, with the parent alert to their baby's feeding rhythms and the signs that she has had enough. Allowing your baby to take her time over her feeds will help both of you to recognise when her hunger has been satisfied. If you watch her carefully, and experiment with taking the teat out of her mouth when her sucking slows right down, you will soon learn the signs that tell you she is ready to stop.

Many people assume that formula feeding means feeds will be (or should be) at regular, fairly long intervals and that the baby will (or should) take the same amount each time. But there is no reason why this needs to be the case; bottle-fed babies are often happier with an approach that allows them to vary how much and how often they eat and, with a bit of trial and error, you will soon find your baby's natural pattern. It won't be fixed, of course, but it will give you some clues as to what her appetite is likely to be at different times of the day.

It's easy for bottle feeding to be shared by many different people, but feeding is a way for your baby and you to communicate on a very intimate and special level. From her point of view she wants to get to know those closest to her, so making feeding something that only you and your partner do, in the early weeks at least, will help to support and nurture the relationships that are most important to her.

'Just after I started using formula I took Chloe to visit my husband's family. When my mother-in-law took her and gave her a bottle, I burst into tears. I was really surprised how important it was to me that I fed her – I'm her mum, feeding was my job, my responsibility. I didn't want that taken away from me.'

Charlotte, mother of Chloe, 10 months

Does my baby need water?

Breastfeeding babies don't need anything other than breastmilk to drink because the consistency of the milk changes as the baby feeds. It tends to be more watery – or thirst-quenching – at first, with bursts of gradually creamier and more filling milk as the feed progresses. This means she can control what she takes according to how thirsty or hungry she is. Although formula remains the same throughout a feed, babies fed on formula don't usually need extra drinks, either, except if the weather is very hot, or if they are ill. If your baby is formula fed and seems to want to feed very frequently (perhaps within two hours of her last feed), you may want to try offering her some cooled boiled water. If she takes it and then seems settled, that's probably what she needed. If she either refuses it or seems to want something else afterwards, then maybe she *is* ready for another feed of formula.

Baby-led breastfeeding – the practicalities

Breastfeeding is all about mother and baby working in sync. The first two weeks are key to getting things going well, to help you avoid problems later. During this time, your milk production is being kick-started and your baby is working out the best way to feed, using her instincts to tell her what to do. The more often she feeds, and the more freedom and gentle support you give her to work out how to do it effectively, the more proficient she will become at attaching to the breast – and the more adept *you* will become at holding her so that she can feed easily. Frequent feeding in the early weeks will also maximise your capacity to make milk for her, both immediately and in the long term. This will give you the best chance of breastfeeding for as long as you both want. This period of frequent feeding is important even if you plan to combine breastfeeding with formula later, because it will make it easier for you to keep breastfeeding going when formula is introduced.

Breastmilk is made on a production-on-demand basis. This means that, as long as your baby is feeding effectively, *she* will regulate how much milk you make, according to her needs. However, if she isn't latched on in the best way, if she is taken off the breast before she's had all she wants, or if there are long gaps between her feeds, your breasts will get the message that less milk is needed and your milk production will start to slow down. This is why it's important not to try to schedule a breastfed baby's feeds or control how long they last.

Here are the essential elements that will get baby-led breastfeeding up and running in the first few weeks. They may also be useful to come back to if you run into difficulties later, especially if you want to increase the amount of milk you are producing:

- **Aim for your baby to feed frequently, day and night** – *at least* eight times every 24 hours in the first two weeks (and probably more, especially if she sometimes doesn't feed for very long) and *at least* six times in every 24 hours after that. If she's sleepy in the early days, or if your breasts feel full, you may need to wake her and encourage her to feed. Try to avoid using a dummy, so that she can signal easily when she wants to feed.
- **Make sure she is feeding effectively.** She needs to be attached to the breast in a way that allows her to get milk easily. After the first few days you should be able to see or hear her swallowing rhythmically while she is feeding – frequently during the main part of the feed and less often towards the end. And feeding shouldn't be painful for you (see box, page 107).
- **Don't give her anything other than your milk**, especially for the first few weeks. Anything else (even water) will

fill her up and make her want less breastmilk – and will reduce your milk production. Bottle feeds of expressed breastmilk are best avoided in the early weeks, too, as teats encourage a different type of sucking, which doesn't work for breastfeeding.

- **Let her feed whenever she wants, and for as long as she wants.** If she has been feeding for a while, she may start to feed more slowly and begin to look quite drowsy, but this is likely to be when she is getting the most creamy milk, which is important for ensuring she feels satisfied and puts on weight (see box, page 103). She will come off the breast when she's ready.
- **Hold her skin to skin as much as possible,** so that she can nuzzle your breast and feed easily whenever she wants to. This will also increase the levels of the hormones that control milk production.

Baby-led breastfeeding, in a nutshell

The acronym FEEDS is a useful way to remember the essentials of baby-led breastfeeding:

- **F**requent – no long gaps, day or night
- **E**ffective – pain-free, and with steady, rhythmic swallowing
- **E**xclusive – baby has only breastmilk
- On **D**emand – whenever she wants (or sooner, if your breasts feel full) and for as long as she wants
- **S**kin to skin whenever possible, especially in the first few weeks

---

Making breastfeeding easy for your baby

There are lots of different ways to hold a baby for breast-feeding but there are a few essential points that are common to all of them. **To get milk effectively, your baby needs to be in a position where she can easily tilt her head back, open her mouth wide and use her tongue to scoop up a large mouthful of breast.** She will find it much easier to do this if you hold her really close to you. Pillows can get in the way – it may be better to wait and see whether you need anything to help you support her before deciding you need a pillow. Check, too, that your clothes aren't making things difficult.

To be able to attach easily your baby needs to have:

- as much of her body in contact with yours as possible (her chest and hips should be touching you; pull her bottom in close and check for gaps)
- her head and body in line (i.e. with her knees facing the same way as her nose)
- her body weight supported (neck, shoulders and hips)
- her head free to move so that she can tilt it back easily
- her arms free to move so she can use her hands to help her
- her nose lined up with your nipple

You'll need to watch for her to open her mouth really wide and then bring her towards you quickly – unless you are in a lying-back position with your baby on top of you (see page 43), in which case she will probably attach without any help. Make sure your hand is supporting her neck and shoulders but *not* touching her head, since this may distract her as well as making it difficult for her to tilt it back (as a guide, check that your fingers and thumb are well below her ears). Her chin and lower lip should touch your breast first, so that her nose stays free. In the early weeks she may bob her head around and use her hands to find the nipple, and take several attempts to attach at the right angle. Once she is latched on and feeding, you may want to wedge a small cushion or

Breastfeeding shouldn't be painful

If breastfeeding hurts, or your nipples seem damaged, get help as soon as possible. Pain usually means that your baby isn't latching on to your breast effectively – the sooner you can help her to change this, the more quickly the problem will be sorted out. She may be finding it difficult because your breast is overfull (engorged). This is most likely to occur in the first week or so, especially if feeding is not very frequent, but it can happen later on if the gap between any two breastfeeds is longer than usual. Hand expressing a little milk will soften your breast and make it easier for your baby to feed.

If at any time you are concerned that breastfeeding isn't going well, ask for help from a breastfeeding counsellor or peer supporter, a lactation consultant (who you may need to pay), a midwife or a health visitor. Alternatively, you might like to go to a breastfeeding support group or call the NHS National Breastfeeding Helpline (see 'Sources of Information and Support', page 229).

rolled-up cardigan under your arm or behind your back, to make yourself comfortable. Let her feed for as long as she wants on the first breast, then offer her the other breast so she can decide whether she wants more.

Breastfeeding out and about

The idea of breastfeeding your baby in public for the first time can be daunting. Many women find that taking along a friend who is breastfeeding, or who has breastfed, can help. Finding parks and cafes where lots of other mothers go – or premises displaying a 'breastfeeding welcome' sign (see 'Sources of Information and Support', page 230) – can make it easier to feel confident to feed in front of other people.

If you're concerned about how much flesh you might expose, you may want to buy a specially designed breast-feeding top – or you could just wear a stretchy, low-cut vest underneath a looser top. Pulling the outer top up and the inner one down will allow your baby to get to your breast without you having to bare your tummy. Many women find that it helps to practise at home in front of a mirror first, so they can work out which clothes are easiest to manage and check how much flesh can be seen. Practising feeding in the dark (or with your eyes closed) at home may also help because it will mean you don't have to watch what you're doing. Then, when you're out, you can just tuck your baby inside your T-shirt or jumper to feed. Alternatively, you could wait until she's latched on, then drape a muslin or shawl over her, or wrap your cardi around you both – or, with a bit of practice, and someone to show you how, you may be able to help her feed inside a sling.

> 'Anna is in the sling almost all the time and I just have my T-shirt pulled up so she can feed whenever she wants. No one can see anything. It's great if you have an older child to care for too, because it means you don't have to stop to feed the baby.'
>
> *Sarah, mother of Ewan, 3 years, and Anna, 3 months*

Baby-led bottle feeding – the practicalities

There are two main challenges for parents who are formula feeding and who want to let their baby lead the way. The first is the need to get the feed ready before the baby starts to become distressed and the second is working out how much formula to prepare. (Letting your baby take the lead during the feeding itself is much easier.) Because formula isn't sterile, it's much safer to prepare feeds freshly each time. So, unless you opt for ready-to-feed formulas, which tend to be expensive, you will

Which type of teat is the best?

There is no 'best' teat for your baby, and no teat feels or works exactly like a breast. Some teats are said to make the baby work 'harder', supposedly to mimic breastfeeding, but breastfeeding isn't harder than bottle feeding – it's just different (in fact, breastfeeding has been shown to involve *less* effort). What matters is that the teat allows your baby to manage the flow of expressed breastmilk or formula without getting frustrated because it's too slow, or having to gulp because it comes too fast. As with bottles, it's simply a case of trying out a few different types and finding out which you and your baby prefer (and which are the easiest to clean).

need to allow at least 10 minutes for making up the feed. This means you need to be alert to your baby's earliest feeding cues so that you can have the bottle ready before she gets distressed. Keeping her very near you will give you the best chance of recognising when she's thinking about asking to feed.

The amounts suggested for each feed on packets and tins of formula are a guide only; your baby's approximate intake in a 24-hour period is more important than how much she has at each feed. Many babies (especially those who have been breastfed or who are having both breastmilk and formula) prefer a pattern that is more similar to breastfeeding, with smaller amounts more frequently.

'She's supposed to be on six bottles a day but I always feed her as often as she wants, so some days it will be more and others, less. She'll just have little feeds whenever she wants them – I never try to get her to finish a bottle. It means I have to have loads of feeding kit with me, though, if I want to be out for a whole day.'

Vicky, mother of Bella, 5 months

How to prepare a formula feed

As powdered formula is not sterile, the feed must be made up with very hot, recently boiled water (over 70°C/160°F) to be sure that any bugs in the powder are killed. The following is the currently recommended procedure:

- Empty your kettle and put at least 1 litre (35 fl oz) of fresh, unboiled tap water into it (bottled or mineral water is *not* suitable). Provided you will be using it within the next 30 minutes, put it on to boil.
- Clean and disinfect the surface you are going to use and wash your hands.
- Check the instructions on the packet or tin and pour the required amount of water into a pre-sterilised bottle. (You can sterilise a bottle by boiling it, or by using a cold water sterilising solution or a steam or microwave steriliser.)
- Add the required amount of powder, filling and levelling the scoop according to the manufacturer's instructions.
- Fit the teat and cap and shake the bottle until everything is thoroughly mixed.
- Hold the bottle under cold running water until the feed is cool enough to give to your baby (test it by tipping a bit on to the inside of your wrist). Use immediately.

If you have to make up a feed in advance (for example, to leave with a babysitter), follow the procedure above, then cool the feed and store it in the back of the fridge for no longer than 24 hours.

Some parents get round the problem of deciding how much formula to prepare by starting with a feed that's on the small side and making up a little more if their baby doesn't want to settle. There will inevitably be some formula left over occasionally, which will need to be thrown away (it's not safe to keep it), but this is likely to get less as you learn your baby's rhythms.

Giving your baby a bottle feed

Like breastfeeding, bottle feeding isn't just about getting a baby fed. There are lots of ways that you can help your baby to feel comfortable, secure and unhurried, so that she can feed in a relaxed way. The following tips should help her get the most enjoyment from her feeds:

(Note: If you have been advised to manage your baby's feeds in a particular way, for example, because she has a weak suck, these points may not all apply.)

- **Hold her close to you,** fairly upright and, with her head supported in a comfortable position. Incorporate a warm, skin-to-skin cuddle if you can.
- **Look at her** and talk to her during the feed. For the first few weeks, until she learns to focus better, she will be able to see you most easily when cradled in your arm.
- **Brush the bottle teat against her nose or upper lip and wait for her to open her mouth wide** before you put the teat in. If you give her enough time, she may even use her tongue to scoop up the teat. This is an important part of helping her to play an active role in the feed, rather than it being done *to* her. It will also help you to avoid inadvertently persuading her to take a feed that she doesn't really need. Encouraging your baby to control her feed this way is especially important if she is breastfeeding as well as formula feeding because it allows her to practise a similar technique to the one she uses to latch on to the breast (although, while she is getting to grips with breastfeeding, it's better to avoid bottles completely if you can).
- **Unless the bottle is designed not to allow air in through the teat, tilt it** just enough to fill the teat with milk (so that when she sucks she gets milk, not a mixture of milk and air), but not so much that it flows too fast.

When she pauses, the milk should stop flowing; if it doesn't, try tilting the bottle slightly less – or switch to a slower-flowing teat.

- **Let her stop feeding briefly, now and then.** This gives her a chance to rest and decide whether she wants any more. Taking the teat out of her mouth when she releases the suction will give her a complete break, and allow her to burp if she needs to. Also, because your baby will probably look at you as she feeds, switching her to your other arm during a pause can help her vision to develop evenly, as well as ensuring equal pressure on the soft bones of her skull.
- **Don't try to persuade her to drain the bottle, or to take any more than she needs,** for example by jiggling the teat in her mouth. Respecting her signals that she's had enough will help to prevent overfeeding and show her you are listening to her.

Recognising when your baby wants to feed

Baby-led feeding relies on being able to understand when your baby is telling you that she needs to feed. She will let you know she is getting hungry through a range of feeding cues (see box, opposite). The earliest of these can be very subtle and easy to miss – she may just murmur in her sleep or flutter her eyelids. Keeping her close to you, night and day, in the early weeks will help you to learn her preferred signals and allow you to respond to her as quickly as possible.

'If my husband is holding Pearl and she wants to feed, she starts knocking her head against his chest, like a woodpecker. If he doesn't give her to me pretty quickly she starts to get really cross, because he's not the one with the milk!'

Janine, mother of Pearl, 3 months

If your baby doesn't get a fairly quick response to her cues to feed, she will probably become increasingly agitated and eventually she'll cry. As explained in the previous chapter, crying is not her primary way of telling you what she needs – it's a sign that means all the other signals she has tried to give have been missed. Crying has evolved as a way to raise the alarm; it's meant to be difficult to ignore, which is why waiting until your baby cries before offering her a feed is quite likely to make feeding more stressful for you as well as her.

How your baby will tell you that she wants to feed

In the first few weeks your baby may display any (or all!) of the following feeding cues as a way of letting you know that she wants to feed:

- Moving her eyes under her eyelids, fluttering her eyelashes
- Turning her head and stretching her neck
- Making little wriggling, squirming and waving movements
- Clenching and unclenching her fists
- Opening and closing her mouth
- Bobbing her head around
- Making kneading movements with her hands
- Making sucking noises or smacking her lips
- Murmuring, whimpering or giving little shouts or cries
- Sucking on her fists or blanket, or on your clothes

Older babies develop their own unique signals, such as rubbing their head against their parent's chest or tensing their body in a certain way. You may be surprised at how quickly you learn to interpret your baby's behaviour – and at how oblivious people around you may be to what she is trying to say.

Crying doesn't just make feeding stressful, it also makes it more difficult. Breastfeeding babies need to be calm if they're to latch on to the breast easily and feed effectively, while bottle-feeding babies who've been crying tend to gulp in air and can end up with painful wind. Babies often swallow air while they are crying, too, meaning they are windy before they even start feeding. It makes sense all round to respond as soon as you can to your baby's requests to feed.

You can offer a feed before your baby asks

You don't always have to wait until your baby asks before you offer her the chance to feed. If you want to go out, for example, and would prefer her to feed before you go, she may be happy to oblige. Or you may just want to have the excuse to sit down and relax for a while. If she's breastfeeding, just brushing your nipple against her nose, and maybe expressing a few drops of milk, will usually be enough to tempt her to feed. If she's formula fed, the smell of the formula and the feel of the teat may have a similar effect.

There may be times when you want your baby to feed because your breasts are beginning to feel uncomfortably full. Having her feed at this point is important to help you avoid conditions such as engorgement and mastitis. Even a baby who is almost asleep will usually be happy to feed just enough to make a difference.

If your baby is very sleepy in the early days – especially if she is jaundiced – or if she is premature or unwell, it may be a good idea *not* to wait until she asks to feed. Frequent feeding (*at least* eight times a day in the first two weeks and *at least* six times a day after that) is important to make sure she gets enough milk and that your breasts are reminded to make more.

Finding your baby's natural pattern

For the first few weeks, at least, your baby will probably want to feed at times that may seem erratic and unpredictable, and bear little relation to night or day. This is normal. After a while you will probably see a rough pattern emerging for the times when she is most likely to want to feed, and for which feeds tend to be the longest. However, this pattern may not be what you expected, and it will almost certainly change as your baby grows and develops. It's also likely to be different on days when she is teething or not feeling well, or is unsettled for some other reason; going on holiday, moving house or family stress can all mean your baby wants to feed or be cuddled more often than usual, just for the reassurance it gives her.

> 'While Belle was teething, she fed all through the night. It was so obvious she needed to feed when she was in pain. As soon as the pain stopped she slept much more.'
>
> *Suzanne, mother of Belle, 3 years*

Babies don't generally choose to feed at evenly spaced gaps throughout the day, although that's what parents are often led to expect. Feeding in lots of short bursts – or clusters – is especially common for breastfed babies, and tends to happen in the evenings. Coping with this can be challenging, but if you go with the flow you will probably find that a bout of cluster feeding is often followed by a longer-than-usual period of sleep. On the other hand, fighting your baby's natural pattern may make her harder to settle. 'Hands-free' breastfeeding, with your baby in a sling, can be helpful if you have lots of other things to do at the same time, such as preparing an evening meal or getting an older child to bed.

'Robin was born at 31 weeks. When he came home I carried him constantly in a stretchy wrap or on my arm – he was so tiny. Around the time of his due date he'd feed about every hour and a half during the day, then feed for about four hours on and off in the evening and then every couple of hours at night. I just went with it and in the evenings I'd just sit back, put a film on and enjoy it. We could see that Robin knew what he needed – my partner would just look at him and say, "He knows what to do!" He soon started to overtake the size of babies born at term!'

Hannah, mother of Robin, 12 months

Why feeding schedules rarely work

Trying to persuade a baby to feed according to a schedule can mean her parents spend a lot of time trying to comfort her (or ignore her crying) when she seems to want to feed at times she 'shouldn't' do. This can make caring for her much harder than it needs to be. It can also affect the amount of milk she gets: if she is breastfed, scheduled feeding risks seriously undermining her mother's milk production, while if she's formula fed, encouraging her to take the same amount at each feed may interfere with her natural ability to control her appetite. Your baby will show you her natural feeding pattern, if you let her.

Feeding your baby at night

All babies need to feed during the night. In the early weeks they are likely to feed more between 7.00pm and 3.00am than they do during the day, and many babies continue to feed through the night once or twice (or more) until they are at least a year old. Sleeping for long stretches without waking *isn't* a natural developmental stage, and not many babies will do it (see page 134 for more on normal sleep patterns).

Many parents find that the key to making night-time feeding easy and ensuring that the whole family gets as much sleep as possible is keeping their baby near them. Sleeping close to your baby means you can respond to her as soon as she stirs, making the time you have to spend awake as short as possible. If you're breastfeeding (and your circumstances make it safe to do so) you may want to have her in your bed with you. This will help you to sense when she begins to stir and will encourage your sleep cycle to get into sync with hers. It will also mean that neither you nor she needs to wake fully for her to feed and you can both drift back off to sleep easily afterwards. (For information on safe bed sharing, see page 150.)

You may find some of these tips help to make feeding easier to cope with at night:

- Time your own bedtime for just after your baby has fed, so you get some rest before she wants to feed again. (An alternative, if you're breastfeeding, is to offer your baby an extra, sleepy feed when you're ready for bed.)
- Keep things quiet and dark in the bedroom. Use the dimmest light you can get away with and talk quietly. This will not only help your baby to wake up slowly and drift off to sleep again easily after feeding but it will also mean she doesn't begin to associate darkness with being hungry or lonely, and light with food and comfort.
- Don't change your baby's nappy at night unless it's very wet, she's done a poo or she's got a nappy rash.
- Relax as much as you can while your baby feeds during the day.
- Try to take a nap while your baby is asleep during the day (see also page 208).

Breastfeeding at night

The following extra tips may help to make breastfeeding easy at night and enable you to get some rest, while still allowing your baby to feed as often as she needs:

- Wear an easy-to-open nightdress, pyjama top or bra, or sleep topless. (If you tend to leak milk, you might want to spread a thick towel underneath your top half, to protect the bed.)
- Have a drink nearby in case you get thirsty, so you don't have to get up.
- Offer your breast as soon as your baby begins to stir, so she doesn't need to wake up fully.

Why giving a bottle doesn't usually help

Many people imagine that giving a baby a bottle during the night, rather than breastfeeding her, will make life easier. This isn't usually true. Bottle feeding (even with expressed breastmilk) tends to be more disruptive during the night, because whoever gives the feed has to wake up fully, both to prepare the feed and to give it safely. Breastfeeding on the other hand, triggers hormones that make both mother and baby drowsy and, once they have got the hang of feeding lying down, many mothers find they are able to do it almost in their sleep (often with no idea, in the morning, how many times their baby fed during the night). Bottle feeding a breastfed baby at night can undermine breastfeeding and may create problems during the day: a long gap between breastfeeds can easily lead to overfull breasts and reduced milk production, and, if the baby is still learning to breastfeed, using a teat can make latching on more difficult for her, so that establishing breast-feeding becomes harder.

- Practise feeding your baby lying down, so you can rest during the feed and drift back to sleep easily afterwards. (*Don't feed your baby on a sofa or in an armchair if you think you may fall asleep because of the risk of her becoming trapped or smothered. A bed is safer.*)
- Practise feeding with your eyes shut during the day so that you don't have to switch on the light at night, which may make it harder for you and your baby to drift back to sleep.

Bottle feeding at night

Bottle feeding at night needs a bit of planning. Unless you are using freshly expressed breastmilk (which can be safely kept at room temperature for up to six hours) or ready-to-use formula, preparing feeds is likely to take some time. Here are a few suggestions for making things quicker and easier:

- Measure the required amount of powdered formula into a clean, covered container before you go to bed.
- Have a kettle ready with some fresh, unboiled tap water, preferably in your bedroom (if it's safe to do so).
- Have a bowl of cold water and perhaps even some ice cubes or a freezer block in a cool bag, ready to cool the feed.
- Mix the powder with half the normal amount of hot, freshly boiled water. Then add the same amount of cooled boiled water, saved beforehand in a sterile bottle. (N.B. It is essential that all the powder is added *before* the cooled water so that the temperature is high enough to kill any bugs.)
- If you don't have to leave your bedroom to prepare the feed, put your baby in your bed while she waits, so the warmth and familiar smell can soothe her.

Baby-led weaning – discovering solid foods

Weaning starts with a baby's first taste of solid food and ends with her last ever feed of breastmilk or formula. This transition takes *at least* six months, and, for breastfeeding babies, it can extend over several years. Just like crawling, walking and talking, learning to eat solid foods is a natural part of a healthy child's development, and, if you allow it to be baby-led, it will happen spontaneously at a time and pace that is right for your child.

Your baby is unlikely to need anything other than breast-milk (or formula) until she's around six months or older. But family mealtimes are social events and there's no need to exclude her just because she is not 'officially' old enough to share the meal. Being allowed to join in, either cradled in your arms or, later, sitting on your lap, will give her the opportunity to watch what's going on and feel part of it all – and it will mean she can start to explore, and then eat, solid foods when she is ready.

By about four or five months your baby will probably be fascinated by the movement of the food from your plate to your mouth and stare intently as you eat. This doesn't mean she is actually hungry, any more than it means she wants to clean her teeth when she watches you cleaning yours, or to make a phone call when she sees you on your mobile. She's just curious. When she's ready to explore a bit more closely she'll begin to reach out and grab food from your plate or the table. By experimenting with it and examining it, she will start to learn about the texture, smell – and possibly taste – of different foods, as well as their appearance. This is the very beginning of the gradual transition from milk feeds to family meals.

How baby-led weaning works

When babies get to around six months old their immune and digestive systems are mature enough to cope with foods other than breastmilk or formula. At the same time they are just beginning to need very small amounts of some micronutrients, such as iron and zinc, in addition to those provided by their milk feeds. Their jaw and mouth muscles are developing, too, as is their ability to sit upright, and they are starting to pick things up and get them to their mouth accurately. All of this means that, by halfway through their first year (or soon after), most babies are ready to start a gradual transition to solid food. The baby-led approach to weaning recognises these developing abilities and skills, and the baby's need to use them to help her learn.

Baby-led weaning (or BLW) is very different from the conventional parent-led approach, in which the decision to start is made by the parents, and in which new foods are puréed or mashed and fed to the baby on a spoon. This is what happens with baby-led weaning:

- The baby is included in family mealtimes, so that she can watch what others are doing and join in when she is ready.
- Nobody feeds her – she starts to handle, explore, play with and eat 'real' food as soon as she is interested and able, using her fingers at first and eventually moving on to cutlery.
- She chooses what to eat, how much and how quickly. There is no pressure to eat a set amount of food or any particular types of food – the emphasis is on allowing her to discover a range of healthy foods in her own time.
- The baby sets the pace for progress with solid foods, handling new textures and tastes spontaneously, as her skills develop.

- She continues to have milk feeds whenever she wants, just as before, and decides when she is ready to reduce them.

To a baby who is starting to explore the world around her, experimenting with food is much the same as trying out a new toy – it doesn't have any meaning for her as a way of dealing with hunger. Gradually, as she discovers how to gum or bite off a piece, she'll experience food inside her mouth, but because the skills she needs to chew and swallow won't develop until a bit later, it will tend to fall back out again. When weaning starts this way, real eating rarely begins before the baby is six, seven or eight months (or even older) – and any food your baby eats will be *in addition to* her milk feeds, rather than replacing them.

> 'I'm not going to have fights about Arnie eating mouthfuls of food he doesn't like. If he wants his yoghurt halfway through his dinner – so what? He goes back to his dinner afterwards. But if we are with family there are a lot of raised eyebrows even though he's got a really healthy attitude to food. He eats a wide range and seems to just know how much he needs.'
>
> Roxanne, *mother of Arnie, 10 months*

Baby-led weaning is a natural progression from baby-led breast- or bottle feeding. It fits with babies' development and is driven by their instincts. It allows them to approach weaning at their own unique pace and to continue to control their own appetite, both for milk and for solid food. All of this helps to keep eating enjoyable, making mealtime battles and stress-related food issues less likely. It also has implications for long-term health and development: research suggests it may play a part in reducing the risk of later obesity, and many parents say handling food this way seems to help with their baby's dexterity. Chewing pieces of food, rather than eating puréed or mashed food, is also thought to help with jaw development.

> 'Breastfeeding led really easily to baby-led weaning. I kept think-ing – surely cavemen didn't purée food? We have created an environment where Florence can take what she needs, and that includes food.'
>
> *Danielle, mother of Florence, 11 months*

Baby-led weaning in practice

As your baby's interest in food grows she may be happy to sit in a high-chair, but there's no need to persuade her to do this if she's not keen; many babies feel more confident on some-one's lap, to begin with. Once she starts handling food, here's how to help her get the most out of it:

- **Include your baby in family mealtimes,** making sure the food is nutritious, avoiding honey and under-cooked eggs, and, as far as possible, added salt, sugar and additives.
- **Choose a time when your baby is not tired or hungry,** so she can relax and concentrate on this new activity.
- **Plan for some mess.** Cover the floor with a large clean cloth or plastic sheet, so that dropped food can be handed back. Things can get quite messy in the beginning, but your baby will quickly become skilled if she's allowed to practise.
- **Cut the food into pieces that she will be able to grasp easily** – roughly adult finger-sized to start with, so there's a bit sticking out of the top of her fist (because she won't be able to open her hand to get at it otherwise). Try thick vegetable sticks, pieces of fruit, strips of meat and fingers of toast. Cook vegetables so they are firm enough to grasp but soft enough to chew.

- **Offer your baby a few pieces of food at a time, preferably from your plate** (so she knows it's safe to eat). You can offer it hand to hand or just put it on the table top or high-chair tray in front of her. Let her play with the food as much as she wants – it's an important part of her learning and enjoyment.
- **Include new shapes and textures,** like rice, minced meat, and runny, crunchy or slippery foods, gradually, alongside foods she can already manage. Aim for a variety of flavours – there's no need for the food to be bland.
- **Keep mealtimes as enjoyable and stress-free as possible** – don't hurry your baby or try to persuade her to eat.
- **Continue to let her have milk feeds whenever she wants** – breastmilk or formula will be her main source of nourishment for some time.

'I'm really tidy and I remember seeing other parents doing baby-led weaning and thinking: "Oh no! There's food everywhere!" But when it came to it, I just couldn't do the whole spoon-feeding thing – it felt so unnatural. And the puréeing seemed to be such hard work. So we've started to eat more healthily and Albert just sits on our laps and joins in. It seems totally natural and easy, and is such an obvious progression from feeding whenever he wants to at the breast.'

Raquel, mother of Albert, 8 months

It's important to let your baby eat at her own pace (if at all); she knows what she needs and how much. Continuing to respect her appetite when she starts solid foods is an important part of helping her to develop a healthy attitude towards food. If she seems interested, let her experiment with drinking water from a small open cup – a shot glass or smooth-rimmed medicine cup will be about the right size – but, if she's breastfeeding, don't be surprised if she prefers to quench her thirst at the breast for several more months.

Safety tips for solid foods

The following guidelines will help to ensure your baby is eating safely:

- Make sure your baby is sitting upright to handle food, not lying back or slumped.
- Don't allow anyone other than your baby to put food into her mouth (beware 'helpful' older children!). This ensures nothing goes in that she is not ready to deal with.
- Don't offer your baby small, hard foods. Cut round foods such as grapes and olives in half and remove any pips or stones. Avoid nuts, whole or in pieces.
- Never leave your baby alone with food.

Some babies gag when they are first learning to handle and chew solid foods. This is not the same as choking; it's more of a retching movement. It can be alarming to watch but it's unlikely to worry your baby. (It can happen with spoon-feeding, too.) A baby's gag reflex is very sensitive – it's triggered a lot further forward on their tongue than an older child or an adult's – probably as a safety feature to prevent food going too far back without adequate chewing. Occasionally a piece of food may go slightly beyond the gag trigger spot, in which case your baby will probably cough it forward. This may make her eyes water a bit but, provided she is not leaning back, she should be able to deal with it easily by herself.

'Chris's mum couldn't quite believe we'd let them feed themselves. It was okay if they were hungry and ate plenty of food, but if they just played with it she'd worry. She was used to spoon-feeding her own kids and knowing exactly how much they'd had. My family just couldn't understand the idea we'd let them put their fingers in the food – they kept saying: "The mess! They aren't eating anything!" But it made perfect sense to us – we knew they were getting whatever they needed.'

Lilly, mother of Ewan, 6, and Dexter, 2 years

What about spoon-feeding?

In most cases, spoon-feeding a baby is simply not necessary – it's a relic from the years when it was believed that babies needed solid foods at three or four months (or even earlier), well before they could feed themselves. For a baby of that age, spoon-feeding is the only option. However, although baby-led weaning works well for most babies of six months and over, there are some babies who need help with eating, alongside the opportunity to feed themselves. Babies who have a disability or developmental delay that prevents them from picking up or chewing food may need to have some puréed meals while they develop the skills necessary to fully feed themselves. Similarly, babies born more than three or four weeks prematurely, or with a specific illness, may need additional nutrients to tide them over until they are able to eat independently. For these babies, a period of spoon-feeding may be needed, either before or in addition to self-feeding, to help support their nutrition while they make the transition to family meals.

Even when there are no problems, some parents occasionally want to use a spoon to feed their baby, for example with runny foods. While many babies are happy to stick their fingers in yoghurt or soup and then suck them, others (and their parents) prefer to use something to scoop with. If you don't mind a bit of mess, you can offer your baby a spoon – or something edible, such as a breadstick or carrot or celery stick – so that she can dip it into the food herself, or you can pass it to her preloaded. On the other hand, if you want to avoid mess (perhaps because you are eating at someone else's house or in a restaurant, and are worried about leaving a trail of devastation from your baby's meal), you may decide to fill and hold the spoon yourself. However, the problem with being spoon-fed by an adult is that it's more difficult for the baby to control what's happening; she can't readily spit something out once it's in her mouth and it's easy for the person feeding her to set too fast a pace without realising, or to encourage her to keep eating after she's had enough. If you need to give your baby some food off a spoon, try to imagine yourself in her place and watch carefully for her cues, so that she can tell you what she wants. She may need time to look at the food and sniff it before tasting it. Letting her hold the spoon or guide your hand as you hold it will allow her more control.

'We use a spoon sometimes, if we're having soup or porridge or something. We load up a spoon and ask if he wants help. Sometimes he'll be kind of falling on to the spoon with an open mouth; other times he'll hold my arm. But we'll only help if he wants us to. If he isn't that bothered he'll just dip his hands in and play with it.'

Bridget, mother of Noah, 9 months

Unless there's a medical reason why your baby needs help to eat, it's important not to try to top her up with puréed or mashed food off a spoon after she has finished feeding herself. There's no need to make sure she's eaten a certain amount or that she's had some of everything. Rather than promoting good nutrition, encouraging her to eat extra this way is likely to lead to overeating, which could become a regular habit, or to make mealtimes into a battle. As long as a range of nutritious food is available and she can have breastmilk or formula whenever she wants, your baby can be trusted to eat what she needs.

Letting go of milk feeds

For the first few months, while any food your baby eats is in addition to her milk, breastfeeding or bottle feeding will simply carry on as before, whenever she asks, rather than necessarily coinciding with family mealtimes. Once she is eating purposefully – which is likely to be from around nine months but may be later – she'll probably begin to cut down the amount of milk she wants. This may result in a change to the number of times she asks to breastfeed or for a bottle, or it may mean that the amount she takes each time gets less. She may simply ask for some of her milk feeds a little later than usual, especially after a meal where she's eaten quite a lot of solid food, meaning that feeds get dropped by themselves. Then, when she is regularly eating at mealtimes, she will probably decide to skip some milk feeds altogether (although this is less likely if she is breastfed, unless she chooses to drink water with her meals). All you need to do is to respond to her cues, just as you have until now.

There's no need for follow-on formula

Formulas marketed as 'follow-on' or 'toddler' milks are *not* necessary, and they may dull your baby's appetite for exploring new foods, limiting rather than improving her overall diet. Formulas described as being 'for hungrier babies', and those that claim to help babies sleep longer, work because they are more difficult to digest, not because they contain more nourishment. There's no need for cow's milk either. Although it can be used as part of a meal from six months – for example, on cereal – it shouldn't be offered as a drink until your baby is over a year old. Breastmilk, or stage one infant formula, is all she needs to ensure good nutrition as she gradually makes the change from milk feeds to family meals.

Babies don't always drop milk feeds steadily and permanently. It's common for them to lose interest in solid foods for short periods, especially when they are teething or fighting off an infection, and to want nothing but milk for a week or two before going back to eating solid foods and taking less milk. If you are breastfeeding, your milk production will naturally fluctuate in response to your baby's demands, but if you are bottle feeding you will need to be alert to these subtle changes in her appetite for milk.

Babies usually continue to rely on breastmilk or formula until they are at least a year old. Allowing your baby to manage her milk feeds as well as the amount of solid food she eats will mean she can negotiate her transition to family meals gradually and safely.

Key points

- Babies are born knowing when they need to feed and how much food they need.
- Baby-led feeding allows your baby to feed according to her instincts and her appetite. It encourages mutual trust and natural appetite control.
- Baby-led feeding revolves around understanding your baby's subtle feeding cues so she doesn't have to wait to feed. This makes feeding less stressful all round.
- Breastfeeding and being baby-led go hand in hand but bottle feeding can be baby-led, too.
- To work well, breastfeeding needs to be Frequent, Effective, Exclusive, on Demand and – where possible in the early days – Skin to skin (**FEEDS**).
- To make bottle feeding intimate and enjoyable, hold your baby close, look at and talk to her, and watch carefully for her signals.

- Your baby's natural feeding pattern will emerge over the first few weeks, although it will remain variable.
- Most babies need to feed during the night; sleeping close to your baby makes feeding easier.
- Breastmilk or stage one formula is all babies need for the first six months and remains the most important part of their diet until they are at least a year old.
- Baby-led weaning helps to prevent mealtime battles and may encourage lifelong healthy eating.
- Baby-led weaning allows your baby to share family mealtimes and feed herself with solid food. It follows naturally from baby-led milk feeding and lets her make the transition at her own pace.
- Allowing your baby to drop her milk feeds in her own time will ensure she is well nourished throughout weaning.

7

Baby-led sleep

A baby-led approach to sleep is a fundamental part of helping your baby to feel nurtured. Nights and nap times are a wonderful opportunity to establish a feeling of security, trust and well-being, which will contribute to his overall health and help to develop a deep and lasting bond between you.

Holding your baby as much as possible while he sleeps, especially in the early weeks, will help him to feel safe in your arms and to associate sleep with feeling close to you, loved and protected. As he grows, and his naps and bedtimes become more distinct, your reassuring presence as he falls asleep and when he wakes up will remind him that you will be there, should he need you. Recognising when he is tired and needs to sleep, and helping him to feel safe while he does so, may help you to avoid the bedtime battles that are so common with toddlers and older children.

This chapter examines why sleep can so often be a stumbling block for parents. It will show you how many of the problems associated with sleep can be prevented by understanding the nurturing that babies really need, and by responding to that need intuitively, led by your baby.

Why is sleep such a problem?

Lack of sleep is one of the bitterest complaints from parents in their baby's first few years. Nights disturbed by children who don't sleep the way their parents expect (or want) are so common that they seem to be an inevitable part of parenting. This suggests that the real problem lies not in what babies actually do but in the mismatch between the way we *think* they should sleep and the way they have almost certainly evolved – and *need* – to sleep.

For generations, parents have been led to believe that babies should sleep through the night from very young – usually by about three or four months old. Indeed, you can pretty much guarantee that, at some point in your baby's first few months, someone will ask you, 'Is he sleeping through yet?' It's easy to feel judged according to your answer, as though you are somehow responsible for your baby's sleep. As a result, many parents feel under pressure to get their child to conform to a pattern that is likely to conflict with his instincts and needs – for example, expecting him to sleep in a room alone, to fall asleep without any help (sometimes known as self-soothing) and to nap at specific times, rather than as dictated by his own internal clock. Goals like these can cause enormous stress in infant–parent relationships because they have no basis in how babies develop naturally or what each baby truly needs.

The myth of 'sleeping through'

Babies aren't meant to sleep for long stretches at night. This false expectation has its roots mainly in a piece of 1950s research carried out in the UK into babies' sleep patterns. In this study, 'sleeping through' was defined as the parents *not being woken* by their baby crying or 'fussing' between midnight and 5.00am. For the baby to qualify as sleeping through he needed to be disturbing his parents between these hours no more than once a week. Waking them before midnight or after 5.00am didn't count. The majority of the parents said that, according to these criteria, their baby was sleeping through by the time he was three months old –

although many reported that he or she later reverted to being more wakeful. Clearly, these results don't tell us very much about the reality of babies' night-time patterns.

It's important to recognise, too, that several features of the way the babies in this study slept (or were reported to have slept) were specific to a particular time and culture – and very different from the way we believe human babies have evolved to sleep. In the UK in the 1950s it was common for babies to sleep in a separate room from their parents, which (since baby monitors hadn't been invented) would have made all but the loudest cries difficult to hear. This means it's quite possible that the babies in the study woke up more often than their parents realised. It was also usual at that time to place babies on their tummies (prone) to sleep, which may have meant they slept more deeply and woke less often than is normal (or safe, see page 135). Formula feeding was gaining popularity at that time, too, so it's probable that most of the babies would have been at least partly formula fed; and, since solids were generally introduced far earlier back then, many would have had cereal as well. Both formula and cereals slow down a young baby's digestion and can contribute to excessively deep sleep.

Even though the way babies of three or four months are cared for at night has changed dramatically in the last half-century, the 'sleeping through' myth has persisted, and, if babies don't do it, the common assumption is that their behaviour constitutes a problem that must be addressed. Over the same period a range of theories has emerged about exactly how many hours of sleep babies need at different ages and how long each period of sleep should be – mostly without considering *where* babies sleep as a factor. All of this puts unnecessary pressure on parents, so that they feel compelled to try to get their baby to fit into a pattern which, in most cases, is likely to be unrealistic.

'The hardest thing when Ethan was a baby was having the wrong expectations about sleep. People tell you how many hours they should sleep and how many naps – but once you start counting it drives you crazy.'

Natasha, *mother of Ethan, 3 years, and Zara, 13 months*

Babies don't sleep like adults

Babies' sleep patterns are very different from those of adults. Newborn babies don't differentiate between night and day – their sleep is unpredictable, spread throughout 24 hours, in lots of short stretches interspersed with (equally unpredictable) times when they want to feed, 'chat', or simply be awake and alert. Very young babies tend to sleep for 16 to 20 hours out of every 24, but they can fall asleep any time of the day or night, just as they did while they were in the womb.

For the first few months of a baby's life there continues to be little difference between a nap and night-time, but very gradually they begin to adapt to the sleeping and waking pattern of those around them. As they grow, their internal body clock adjusts to cycles of day and night and they start to sleep for longer periods at night, with fewer naps during the day. This happens at a pace that is right for the individual baby – it can't be rushed. Most children take several years to have all their sleep at night, with no daytime nap, and in many cultures at least one nap – or siesta – continues to be enjoyed by both children and adults. Historically, and still in some societies today, it was usual for adults to sleep for only about four hours at a time, and to get up in the middle of the night to work or socialise. In fact research suggests that shorter night-time sleeps, and napping whenever we need to, probably makes biological sense for all of us, leading to better health and greater productivity than the single long sleep that is expected in modern-day Western culture.

'I go to bed at the same time as Madison in the evening, so I can sleep when she has her longest stretch of sleep. She's always more wakeful between midnight and 5.00am so, rather than fighting it and then trying to keep up my normal sleep patterns, I just decided to go with what's easy. She's 12 weeks now and I'm getting plenty of sleep, and my partner's happy with it – he doesn't get disturbed much. We know it won't last forever.'

Laura, mother of Madison, 3 months

Understanding how sleep works

Both adults and babies sleep in cycles that include two types of sleep: active sleep – known as REM or rapid eye movement sleep – and quiet sleep. Quiet sleep starts off light and gradually deepens. During REM sleep our brains are busy, dreaming and processing the information that we have taken in during the day. During quiet sleep our conscious brain is switched off so it can recharge itself. For the average adult, each cycle of sleep lasts around 90 minutes, beginning with quiet sleep and ending with REM. We have more quiet sleep in each cycle in the first half of the night but as morning approaches REM takes over – so we drop off into deep sleep first and then dream more as the night progresses.

Babies have shorter, more active sleep cycles, dominated by REM, and they are more likely to wake up fully between cycles. Their cycles are about 60 minutes long, on average, and begin with light, REM sleep, moving into quiet sleep about 20 minutes later, then back into REM sleep again. During quiet sleep your baby will appear to be fast asleep and will be quite floppy – this is when he can be moved most easily without waking. During REM sleep, however, he'll twitch and murmur and wake readily. A short sleep cycle is important for babies, so they can wake easily if their breathing slows down or they become overheated – encouraging them to spend too long in quiet sleep can put them at risk.

Waking at night is normal, even for adults. As each sleep cycle ends we tend to wake up briefly and turn over, snatching back the duvet or reaching for a drink before going back to sleep. Often, we don't remember these wakeful periods and wrongly assume that we have slept soundly all night. What makes the difference between waking in the morning feeling rested, and waking feeling tired or grumpy, isn't *whether* we've woken during the night but *when*. Waking naturally between sleep cycles isn't a problem – but being woken in the middle of a sleep cycle can be. And the different-length sleep cycles of babies and adults means that, unless your baby sleeps very close to you (when your sleep cycles can become synchronised, see page 147), it's quite likely you'll be right in the middle of one of your sleep cycles when he wakes naturally at the end of one of his.

It isn't necessarily hunger

Young babies need to feed as often at night as they do during the day, especially if they are breastfed; so when they wake it's mostly because they're hungry. But older babies wake at night for many different reasons – for example, a full bladder, a vivid dream or an unusual noise can all cause a baby to wake – especially at the end of a sleep cycle. Just like an adult, once the baby is awake he may decide he is thirsty, or a bit peckish. Or he may just want the soothing quality of a feed to help him get back to sleep. This doesn't necessarily mean he isn't getting enough to eat or drink during the day – even if he has suddenly become more wakeful after a few weeks of sleeping for longer. Encouraging a formula-fed baby to drink extra amounts of formula just before he goes to sleep, or introducing solid food before the baby is really ready, may well slow down his digestion but it won't necessarily mean he stays asleep. In fact, research shows that, for some babies, giving them food they don't need leads to *more* disturbed sleep.

Your baby's pattern – finding it, not fighting it

As a newborn, your baby will be drifting in and out of sleep all day and all night, and waking frequently to feed. There probably won't seem to be much sense to it all, except that feeding and sleeping will tend to be linked. As he gets older, and you begin to recognise his rhythms, his own unique pattern of sleeping, waking and feeding will emerge and you'll begin to be able to predict when his tired times are and how long his naps are likely to last. This is when many families find their day starts to fall into a recognisable (baby-led) routine. However, your baby's sleeping pattern will continue to evolve and change as he grows – and there will be frequent variations, too. For example, if he is poorly or teething he may revert to sleeping more in the day and less at night. And you can expect any big change, such as a house move or his mother going back to work, to affect his sleep, just until he gets used to the new situation.

'My first daughter only ever had half-hour naps and I was so anxious because I thought babies were supposed to sleep for longer – the book I'd read said anything under 45 minutes wasn't a proper nap. I thought there was something wrong with her, or that it was somehow my fault. But my second baby is the same – she wakes up after half an hour whether she is in my arms, the sling, the buggy or the bed. I finally realised it was just their normal pattern.'

Alex, mother of Jessica, 5 years, and Grace, 6 months

During the day and in the evening, learning your baby's signs of tiredness will help you to recognise when he wants to sleep and to work out the sorts of things that may help him to drop off – or that are likely to stop him from sleeping. This will help you to anticipate his needs. For example, he may be telling you he's tired if:

- his activity level slows down
- he goes very quiet or starts making whimpering noises
- he yawns
- he looks a bit 'glazed over', or seems to be staring at nothing
- his eyelids are starting to droop
- he looks as though his head is too heavy for him to lift
- he begins to get grumpy or to cry easily
- he's asking to feed

The sooner you can respond to these subtle cues, the easier it will be to help him fall asleep. Allowing him to become overtired, on the other hand, will make it harder for him to relax and may make falling asleep more difficult. As you get to know your baby's natural pattern you'll be able to predict when he may be ready for a nap or bed, which will help you to plan your day so he can sleep when he needs to.

Why sleep schedules rarely work

Routines that are based on anything other than an individual baby's natural rhythms can be hard work for parents to impose and are unlikely to work long term. For example, keeping a tired baby awake because it's not 'time' for his nap (or in an effort to make him sleep longer at night) is very likely to backfire, with him becoming more and more unhappy as his need for sleep increases. When the appointed time finally arrives he may well be so overtired that he is almost impossible to calm, even though what he now desperately needs is sleep. Schedules can also interfere with the day-to-day flexibility that most families want and need, because doing anything out of the ordinary risks disturbing the baby's routine. For instance, if a baby sleeps during a long car journey when he would usually have been awake, he may not be ready to sleep when his scheduled nap or bedtime comes around.

Parents who are trying to establish a set routine for bedtimes (or who are just desperate for more sleep) are sometimes advised to let their baby 'cry it out'. This can be stressful for them *and* their baby, and many abandon it because they find it impossible to ignore their child when he is so obviously unhappy. Some parents report that this approach worked for them, although they often say the effect wasn't long-lasting. This isn't surprising: if they are left long enough, most babies *will* stop crying (this is thought to be a mammalian survival response, which prevents a baby who has been left alone from attracting the attention of predators). However, research suggests that when this happens the baby can be left with high levels of the stress hormone cortisol in his system. In other words, although he may appear to have 'soothed himself', in reality he is still stressed. If he is repeatedly left to stop crying without being comforted he may find it increasingly hard to calm down fully.

'My kids never had set nap times or bedtimes. When they were babies, we'd go out every day and they would sleep as and when they needed to – in the sling, pram, buggy or car – and now they're much older they're all still able to crash anywhere and have a lie-in at the weekend to catch up after a busy week. Friends have commented that our children are easy-going and don't turn into overtired monsters when they're up late at parties. It suits us to have a busy social life in which babies and children are included. It's nice not to have to rush home and pay a babysitter!'

Claire, mother of Flora, 17, Nancy, 14,
Maud, 12, and Agnes, 10 years

Where should my baby sleep?

Ideally, your baby should sleep very close to you – within touching distance, if possible. In terms of human history, the practice of putting babies in a separate room to sleep – either at night-time or for naps during the day – is very recent, and doesn't reflect what babies need. Even when we're asleep we're aware of our surroundings, and we sleep better if we feel safe. For a young baby, feeling safe means knowing someone is there, and that means being able to hear them, smell them – or, better still, touch them. Being on his own (or feeling as though he's on his own) may make it difficult for him to sleep. Many parents want to be close to their baby, too, and find it difficult to relax unless they can see him or hear his movements and murmurs. Some say they don't feel complete without being able to touch their baby, especially in the early months.

In a sense, this isn't surprising. Research shows that the presence of an adult helps to keep young babies safe while they sleep, and that sleeping alone is one of the factors that increases the risk of sudden infant death syndrome (SIDS, also known as cot death). This is why it's recommended that babies under six months should be in the same room as an adult when they are asleep, both at night-time and during the day. This doesn't mean, though, that babies *over* six months should be put into their own room – the six-month marker simply reflects the fact that the risk of SIDS gets less as babies get older. Many parents report that their children continue to get more sleep when they are near them, well into their toddler years and beyond.

How close should my baby be?

Having your baby in the same room with you means you can respond to him quickly if he needs you; it also means he doesn't have to call out to know you are there. Just being aware of your presence may sometimes be enough to help him move from one sleep cycle to the next without help. However, when he's very young, being on the other side of the room from you may not be quite close enough for him. A very young baby hasn't yet learnt to differentiate between things he can see and hear in the distance and those that are close to him. The only way he knows his mother or father is there is if he can feel and smell them.

Many parents have found that their baby sleeps much better if he is within touching distance of them than if he is even a few feet away. Research suggests that sleeping close to an adult can help to regulate a baby's breathing, reducing the risk of the rate slowing down too much during sleep (this is known as apnoea, a condition commonest in the first few months). The feeling of safety that being close promotes also tends to maintain the baby's stress hormones at a low level, helping his digestive and immune systems to function effectively, as well as keeping him relaxed.

Keeping your baby within touching distance of you when he's asleep as well as when he's awake can help you to become attuned to one another much more quickly. Many parents find they rapidly develop almost a 'sixth sense' for when their baby needs them, through a heightened sensitivity to the subtlest of his signals and patterns. Keeping your baby close while he sleeps will also mean you get to know the movements and noises he makes naturally, which *don't* necessarily mean he's waking up (and which you'll quickly learn to sleep through) – and it will give you advance warning when he *is* surfacing. All of this can make parenting at night easier and more intuitive.

Keeping your baby close for daytime sleeps

The best place for your baby to sleep is where he is happy, safe and can stay asleep for as long as he needs to. It may be a case of trying a few different options to see what works

Tip for moving a sleeping baby

If your baby has fallen asleep and you want to move him, wait until he goes into a deep sleep (when he seems floppy – usually about 20 minutes after he's fallen asleep), when he will be less likely to wake easily. If you are putting him down in a cot, buggy or bed, warming the surface a little beforehand (for example, with a hot water bottle) will help to prevent him waking up.

best for you both. Many families find that in the first couple of weeks their baby is happiest sleeping in the arms of one of his parents, against their chest or nuzzled into their shoulder, but that his preferences then change and fluctuate as he gets older. For example, your baby may sleep really well in a sling for a few weeks or months, then suddenly prefer to be lying on a bed with you or even on a blanket on the floor, and then want to go back to the sling again. It may also be different on days when he is unwell or teething. Babies vary, too, in their preferences for noise, with some liking a quiet atmosphere and others sleeping better when there's a bit of background activity. Your baby is the best judge of where he feels most comfortable – and you are the best judge of how to fit that in with your life so that you and he are both happy.

Staying flexible about nap-time arrangements will help you to adapt as your baby grows and develops, and his needs change. Even if you prefer to be at home at the times he is likely to be tired, it may be a good idea to give him the chance to get used to sleeping in other situations, too, so that unexpected changes don't worry him.

'Joe and Dylan slept together in a Moses basket when they were tiny. I think it helped them to get a pattern together because I noticed that the times when they woke up to feed gradually got closer together. Now I feed them to sleep in bed and then they go into their own cots next to our bed but they often come back into the bed for a while, for warmth and cuddles.'

Karen, mother of Joe and Dylan, 2 years

Is a baby monitor a good idea?

A baby monitor allows parents to be in a different room while still being able to hear (or see) their infant. Having a monitor means you can respond to your baby when he starts to wake from sleep almost as quickly as you could if he were in the same room as you. What it doesn't do, though, is provide him with the same sort of reassurance that it gives you. Some parents have found, even when they have a monitor, that their baby can quickly become distressed when he wakes in another room, simply because he can't see them when he opens his eyes, or hear them when they call out to let him know they're coming.

Monitors don't actually keep babies safe, either – even the type that detects movement as well as noise (sounding an alarm if the baby has been still for too long) has not been shown to reduce the risk of SIDS, whereas research suggests that the physical presence of another person close by *can* help to protect babies.

Keeping your baby close for sleep at night

Night-times with a baby can be hard work, especially in the early weeks, when you are getting used to one another and sorting out feeding at night. Being close to your baby can help. Welcoming him into your bed, or having his cot right up close to you, will help him to associate night-time with comfort and protection, and make responding to him easier. Many parents have found that making the decision to have their baby sleeping as close to them as is possible and safe (see page 150) is the secret to nourishing, restful sleep for the whole family.

Cot sleeping versus bed sharing

Sleeping arrangements can vary enormously – from family to family, from child to child and from night to night. Some parents know from the outset that they want to share their bed with their baby; others won't even entertain the idea. Still others start out intending to use a cot but find that bed sharing is easier. Some put their baby into a cot for part of the night and have him in their bed the rest of the time; others use a cot on some nights but not on others. And some parents fall asleep unintentionally with their baby in their bed, just because tiredness takes over. Many families find they end up using a combination of cot sleeping and bed sharing at different times, depending on where their baby settles best and where they feel happiest with him sleeping. And research shows that most babies get taken into their parents' bed at least occasionally – especially if they are breastfed. However, there are circumstances in which bed sharing *isn't* advisable (see page 150), which means it's a good idea to think about your sleeping arrangements ahead of time, to ensure that your baby will be safe every night.

Many health professionals are wary of recommending bed sharing because research suggests it may increase the risk of the baby coming to harm, as compared with cot sleeping. The risks connected with bed sharing are related mainly to smoking, alcohol intake and drug use, as well as to features of the bed itself. However, the information that is given to parents can be confusing because not all the available research deals equally with these various factors – and some doesn't differentiate between co-sleeping on a sofa (which has been shown to be very dangerous) and co-sleeping in a bed, which carries far fewer risks. An understanding of the risks associated with both cot use and bed sharing will help you to make the best choices for you and your baby.

> 'I had it in my head that the baby is in your room until six months and then they should go into a cot in their own room. So that's what we did. I tried feeding her to sleep and then putting her in the cot. It lasted about a month until I realised it was pointless getting up all the time – I was completely exhausted. No one was getting much sleep, so she's back in our bed.'
>
> *Kim, mother of Alice, 10 months*

Using a cot

Cot sleeping was unusual in the majority of families until the late 19th century. Until then, as is still the case in most of the world today, most babies simply slept with their mother. The gradual move towards general cot use was driven by three main factors: the high infant mortality rate, which was blamed on the spread of disease through close contact; the high rates of babies being 'overlaid' (i.e. smothered, sometimes deliberately) in the parental bed, especially in poorer families; and the increasing medicalisation of birth, which involved the use of drugs that left mothers unable to look after their baby safely, requiring them to be cared for by someone else for the first few days. Using a cot meant not only that the baby was less likely to be within touching distance of his mother but also that he could be put into a separate room to sleep. By the middle of the 20th century, cots were in widespread use throughout the UK.

Using a cot doesn't mean that your baby has to sleep a long way away from you. Having the cot as close as possible to the side of your bed will mean that he can sense your presence and you can touch him (and, ideally, pick him up) without having to get out of bed. A co-sleeper, clip-on cot – also known as a side-car cot – will bring him closer still and

Safe sleeping

Wherever your baby sleeps, it's important to keep him as safe as possible. Make sure any equipment conforms to British safety standards and is assembled and used correctly; it's recommended that second-hand cots are fitted with a new mattress for each baby. The following precautions will minimise risks; unless specified, they apply to all sleeping situations. (N.B. 'Cot' means a cot or a Moses basket.)

- Make sure the mattress is firm and the sheets are tight-fitting. A saggy mattress or waterbed could cause your baby to end up in a dip.
- Remove extra pillows, spare covers, cot bumpers and soft toys. Babies don't need their own pillow until they are around a year old.
- Make sure there are no cords or curtains that could become entangled with your baby.
- Make sure the cot, or the side of the bed where your baby will sleep, is not next to a radiator.
- Make sure your baby isn't overdressed (he doesn't need any more layers than you wear for sleep) and there's nothing that could cover his head. In a cot, a low-tog baby sleeping bag or light blankets will be safer than a duvet.
- *Always* lay your baby on his back to sleep, not on his tummy or side.
- In a cot, lay your baby with his feet at the foot of the cot, so he can't wriggle down under any covers.
- Don't allow pets in or on the bed or cot, even if your baby isn't there.
- Make sure nobody smokes in any room where your baby sleeps, whether or not he is there at the time.
- If your baby is under six months old, stay in the same room as him while he is asleep. This applies for daytime naps and at night.

is a handy compromise between a separate cot and sharing a bed. A cot like this has three closed sides and one open one, designed to fit closely against the edge of your bed so that its surface is continuous with your own mattress. This means you can reach your baby easily and slide him nearer to you for feeding. If you're using a side-car cot, make sure it's securely attached to your bed and there is no gap that could trap your baby's limbs between the two surfaces.

Bed sharing

Sharing your bed with your baby is the most obvious way of keeping him close enough to touch at night and, if he's breastfeeding, it's a real advantage when it comes to night-time feeding. In fact, research shows that, where baby and mother sleep together, breastfeeding goes on for longer. It's also a great way to reconnect with your baby if you have to be apart during the day, or if either of you has had a stressful day. Parents who work long hours outside the home often say how much they value spending night-times with their baby.

There are many potential benefits to sharing your bed with your baby. Here are just some of them:

- **Your sleep cycles can synchronise with your baby's.** Although adults and babies naturally have different-length sleep cycles, an adult's cycle isn't fixed. Over time, an adult who sleeps in close proximity to a baby naturally changes their sleep cycle to come into line with the baby's. The closer your baby is to you at night, the more likely you are to be nearing the end of a sleep cycle at the same time as he is. This means you are less likely to have to wake up from a deep sleep to respond to him, so you'll feel more rested in the morning.
- **Breastfeeding will be easier.** Being able to offer your baby a feed as soon as he wakes, and without anyone

needing to get out of bed, means everyone's night is less disturbed.

- **Your baby's temperature will be regulated.** Young babies can easily become overheated or chilled because they aren't good at keeping their core (internal) body temperature steady. Close body contact will enable you to check your baby's temperature easily and to respond quickly if he seems too warm or too cold. Breastfeeding mothers, in particular, have been shown to spontaneously adjust the covers around their baby to warm or cool him without either of them waking up. Sleeping skin to skin is even better, because it allows the baby's temperature to be directly regulated by the parent's body. (Note that the risk of overheating comes from the baby's clothes and the bedclothes, which will tend to prevent him losing heat, not from the parent's body.)

- **Your bond with your baby will increase.** The low-level communication that happens during sleep when parent and baby are close means they get to know each other on an intuitive level, allowing their bond to be strengthened and cemented in their non-waking hours as well as their shared awake times.

- **Everyone will get more sleep.** If you are nearby throughout the night, your baby is less likely to have to wake up fully or cry loudly to get your attention. And knowing you will be able to respond immediately if he needs you may make it easier for you to relax and sleep peacefully, too. A shared sleeping environment can also make it more likely that a baby who is inclined to wake up early in the morning can be persuaded to go back to sleep for another hour or two!

- **It's enjoyable!** Most people enjoy sleeping close to the people they love – many parents who have shared a bed with their baby say they look back on it as a special, precious time.

Bed sharing doesn't have to mean no sex

Many couples who share a bed with their baby find they become more inventive about where and when they have sex, but babies who are used to being where there is movement and noise are rarely disturbed by it. If you prefer, you can put your baby in a cot or on a mattress on the floor beside you. If you help him fall asleep there, or put him down gently soon after he's fallen asleep, you'll have the best chance of a reasonably long period without interruptions.

It's important that your baby has room to move when he's in your bed. If you are sleeping on your own with him, you may find a double bed works better than a single one. Many families find that, where both parents and two or more children will be sharing, a king-sized bed is best, provided there is enough room for it. An alternative is to have two mattresses on the floor (either two singles, two small doubles, a double and a single, or a double and a cot mattress). If you can, have the smaller mattress against the wall (so it can't move) or use a large sheet over both of them, to prevent them from coming apart.

'The best thing we ever bought was a super-king-size bed. It had an immediate positive impact on everyone's sleep. Caitlin could be in with us and we all had enough space. And, now she's older and has a little sister, if she wants to come into our bed, there is room for the four of us, just about, to be comfortable. We have the baby in a little sleeping bag in the middle and my partner and I have separate single duvets, so there's no fighting over a shared duvet and less chance of it getting pulled over her.'

Carla, mother of Caitlin, 5 years, and Phoebe, 11 months

Safe bed sharing

Babies have slept next to their parents for thousands of years but modern adult beds and lifestyles haven't been designed with babies in mind. For this reason, bed sharing sometimes carries different risks from cot sleeping. The information below is based on the latest research and will help you to keep your baby safe while he's in your bed:

- Check that your baby can't get trapped or injured between the mattress and the headboard or wall, and that he can't fall off the bed. (A mattress on the floor with no headboard may be safer than an ordinary bed.)
- If there is an older child in the bed, make sure an adult sleeps between the older child and the baby. If the older child is likely to come into the bed during the night, make sure he or she knows where in the bed they should sleep.
- Until your baby is old enough to find his own position in the bed, sleep on your side, curled round him, with his head at the level of your chest. This will keep him from going into the pillows or being lain on. If you are breastfeeding, lying like this will allow him to feed easily and to roll on to his back to sleep afterwards.
- Make sure your baby can move his limbs freely; babies should never be swaddled (see page 156) when sharing a bed.
- Never leave your baby in or on your bed on his own unless you are in the same room and aware of his movements.

Research to date shows that bed sharing is NOT safe if:

- the baby's mother smoked during pregnancy *or* anyone sharing the bed is currently a smoker
- anyone sharing the bed might not be able to respond normally to the baby, for example, if they are ill or drunk (having consumed

enough alcohol to make them unsafe to drive a car is a useful rough guide), or have taken recreational drugs or something that could make them sleep unusually deeply

There is some evidence that bed sharing *may* be less safe if:

- the baby is not breastfed or is not sharing the bed with his mother (existing evidence suggests that breastfeeding mothers sleep with their babies in a particularly safe way)
- anyone sleeping right next to the baby is so tired that they may not be able to respond normally to the baby (this is generally reckoned to be the case for someone who has had less than four hours' sleep in the past 24 hours)
- the baby was born prematurely

'My partner's mum was always making comments about us bed sharing – that he'd be in our bed at 18 and stuff. He was only three months old! When we stayed with her she offered us a cot for him. But she came in one morning with a cup of tea and saw the three of us in bed all snuggled up and just said, "I totally get it now. It's beautiful."'

Becky, mother of Fred, 1 year

Moving on from bed sharing

There is no 'right' time for a child to move out of his parents' bed; each family – and each child – is different. All children move into their own bed at some point, especially if their bedroom is somewhere they feel happy. However, if you find you are ready for your child to leave your bed sooner than he is, he'll need your help to make the transition.

If you are not enjoying sharing your bed

Some families find that bed sharing is sometimes less comfortable than they'd hoped. If you aren't enjoying having your baby in your bed, the reason may be one of the following:

- **The bed is too small** (or your baby is a wriggler): If there's not enough room for everyone to stretch out, try putting two mattresses together on the floor (see page 149).
- **Your baby feels too far away**: If your bed is very big, your baby may keep waking up because he feels 'lost' in it. Try moving him closer to you.
- **Your baby wants to breastfeed almost all the time**: Sleeping close to a breast all night can prove irresistible to some babies. If this is bothering you, having your partner sleep next to the baby for some or all of the night may help.
- **Your baby is noisy**: This is most likely to be a problem in the early weeks, before you have got used to the snuffles and grunts your baby makes.

When the problem is something that can't easily be solved, some couples opt for one of them to sleep in another bed for all or part of the night, while others find that having their baby in a cot or a mattress on the floor beside their bed offers the best compromise.

If you do decide to move your baby out of your bed it's a good idea to have a plan for where he will sleep and what you will do when he wakes in the night (as he almost certainly will, even if he has apparently been sleeping through in your bed). Older babies who are used to being in their parents' bed often dislike being in a cot, so your baby may be happier on a mattress on the floor. This will also mean you can lie down beside him to help him fall asleep – and, once he can crawl, he'll be able to climb off the mattress safely and come and find you, so he won't need you to go to him when he wakes.

> 'They all left our bed when they felt ready – but, even now, most mornings I'll wake up with the youngest next to me. I love it when we are on holiday and we all sleep in one big room. I feel like a lioness with my cubs around me. I always sleep so well when I can hear them all breathing and know they are all safe, close to me.'
>
> Daniela, mother of Eva, 11, Stanley, 8, and Joe, 5 years

Helping your baby to fall asleep

Babies don't need to be taught to sleep. As long as the conditions are right for them, and they are ready to sleep, they will fall asleep whenever, and for as long as, they need. Some babies fall asleep easily, whoever they're with and wherever they are. Others need help to relax and drift off, even when they are showing signs of being tired.

Parents use a range of things to help their baby to get to sleep, which evolve as the baby gets older and they become more attuned to his rhythms and preferences. In general, the easiest way to help a newborn baby to fall asleep is to remind him of when he was in the womb. His mother's heartbeat, the sound of her voice, and being held close to her will all help to recreate the feeling of being inside her. Most babies find feeding soothing, too, which is why so many parents choose to let their baby feed himself to sleep. If your baby seems relaxed and sleepy when he finishes feeding, there's no need to wind him. If you continue holding him close, sleep will usually follow naturally.

'I had a book that said you should wake the baby up after a feed. It doesn't make sense – who wants to wake a sleeping baby? I wish I'd known to trust my instincts – that it was okay to relax and let him stay asleep.'

Maja, mother of Alexander, 5 years, and Maria, 11 months

The following are some tried-and-trusted ways of helping a tired baby to fall asleep; they can work for both naps and night-times, either individually or in combination. Trying a few, and listening to your baby, will help you to discover what works best for him:

- Feeding
- Being rocked or swayed gently in your arms
- Being held while you dance to soothing music
- Being carried in a sling
- Being held skin to skin
- Lying on your chest, or snuggled into your neck – many babies particularly like the feel of their father's chest (sleeping tummy-down on someone's chest *doesn't* carry the same risks as prone sleeping in a cot or bed, provided the adult is awake)
- Being massaged or stroked gently and rhythmically
- Lying down beside you in bed, especially if you are falling asleep (or pretending to!)
- Being sung to, especially soothing lullabies
- Listening to soothing music, or birdsong
- Listening to white noise or 'womb music', for example:

  ○ Repeated 'shhh' sounds, in a gentle voice
  ○ The sound of wind in the trees, the sea running over pebbles or a babbling brook
  ○ The sounds made by dolphins or whales
  ○ The noise of a tumble dryer

- Sucking on a dummy (but see box, opposite)

- Being taken for a walk outdoors in a sling or buggy
- Being taken for a ride in the car

Most babies fall asleep more easily if they are being held, and the rocking motion of walking or swaying usually helps them to drift off quickly, too. Some parents 'wear' their baby in a sling for most of the day, which works particularly well for newborns because it means they can sleep whenever they want to. Others put their baby into the sling when he starts to become tired, either keeping him there, or (if he's getting heavy) laying him down once he's dropped off.

Of course, all babies are different. Just as some like quiet and others prefer some noise, some find rocking or stroking soothing when they're tired while others are irritated by it. Some go through phases when they don't want to be held at all, apparently finding it hard to relax until they are put down. The more open you can be to what works best for your baby, the easier it will be to help him settle.

What about using a dummy?

Sucking on a dummy can help a baby to fall asleep because it acts as a substitute for suckling at the breast. However, babies can become reliant on dummies very quickly, and regular use may lead to problems (see page 80). There has been speculation that there may be a connection between dummies and safer sleep, especially when babies sleep alone. It's thought this may be because sucking (whether at the breast or on a dummy) may help prevent the extended periods of deep sleep that are otherwise a risk. However, this has not been proven and dummy use isn't part of current infant sleep recommendations.

Helping your baby to settle without needing to be held

Some parents find that, although their baby might enjoy being close to them while he falls asleep, they'd like him to learn to fall asleep without needing to be held, especially as he gets older. Helping your baby to associate something else with the sensation of relaxing and drifting off can be an effective way to do this. For example, stroking him in a rhythmic way, making soothing sounds, playing music or singing to him while you hold, cuddle, rock or feed him will help him to link the two things together. If you always stroke him the same way, and use the same sounds, music or singing (choose something you can bear to hear or sing over and over again!), over time you will find he'll be able to fall asleep with these sensations on their own. This won't happen immediately – it could take several months – but it's a gentler (and probably longer lasting) alternative to sleep-training techniques that involve leaving a baby to cry.

Swaddling isn't recommended

Swaddling – that is, when a baby is wrapped in a shawl, sheet or blanket so that his arms are held against his sides or across his front – is sometimes used to help babies to fall asleep on their own, and to stay asleep for longer. However, swaddling can lead to over-heating (even if the covering is thin and the baby's head is uncovered) because it prevents the baby from opening his arms to cool himself. It has also been linked to a higher incidence of SIDS, possibly because the sheet or blanket restricts the baby's breathing, or because the baby is encouraged to fall into a deeper sleep than is safe. Recent research also suggests very tight swaddling around the legs and bottom may increase the risk of dislocated hips.

'Matilda would cry after she'd finished a breastfeed and I didn't know what to do. My mum was visiting one day and suggested that she might be tired and might want to be put down to sleep. I thought this was unlikely: my first daughter had hated being put down and would only sleep on me or my husband or with us in bed. Still, I put Matilda into the pram and, sure enough, she was soon asleep. We'd had a Moses basket for Eliza, but she would never sleep in it and by the time Matilda was born we'd given it away. We borrowed a crib and she slept happily in that in our bedroom and only came into our bed for feeds. Clara and Frankie both wanted to be close to us at night, just like Eliza.'

Teresa, mother of Eliza, 9, Matilda, 7, Clara, 5, and Frankie, 2 years

Bedtime routines for older babies

Once your baby is beginning to have his longest sleep in the early part of the night, a bedtime routine may provide a comforting, reassuring and relaxing end to the day. This can help to give a sense of a 24-hour rhythm, and – providing he's showing signs of being tired (without which the best winding-down routine in the world is unlikely to work) – will probably help relax him into sleep.

'Having a bit of a routine helped me feel better about her sleep when she was little, so I always closed the curtains every evening and opened them every morning, even if her sleep didn't coincide with those times. She'd always have a bath too. I didn't stick to a time though – I'd wait until she seemed tired. If things are difficult it's easy to feel you should be able to sort it out, but it didn't last forever – she just slept better as she got older.'

Emma, mother of Rosy, 18 months

Here are some of the things that can work well as part of a bedtime routine. It may take a little trial and error to find the ideal combination for your baby:

- A calm, quiet atmosphere in the house (this can be difficult to achieve if you have older children; you may need to enlist your partner's help)
- Some skin-to-skin time
- A warm bath (taking your baby into *your* bath will mean you get skin-to-skin contact, too)
- Being put into warm night clothes
- Low lights and closed curtains
- Soft music, womb sounds or lullabies
- A gentle massage (see page 187)
- Listening to you talk about what happened during the day, or your plans for tomorrow (even a young baby will enjoy the sound of your voice)
- Sharing a book or listening to a story
- Having a leisurely feed
- Having an extended cuddle

Bedtime can be any time that suits your child – lots of older babies are ready for their main stretch of sleep by 7.30pm or earlier, but there are some whose natural rhythm is to stay awake well beyond this and then sleep later in the morning. Your baby's pattern may not be the same every day, either: an unusually busy day may mean he is ready for bed earlier than usual – or it may mean he fits in a late-afternoon nap and is not ready to start his long sleep until well into the evening.

'We don't really put Maya to bed before we go to bed. She's usually on and off the breast in the evening until she finally goes to sleep snuggled against my chest, or my partner's. The noise doesn't seem to bother her and we love having her there close to us. So we just put our feet up and watch the telly while she sleeps; then we all go to bed together.'

Gita, mother of Maya, 5 months

Key points

- Babies' sleep patterns and their night-time needs are different from those of adults.
- Keeping your baby close to you by day and at night means you can respond to him quickly and will help to keep him safe.
- Babies expect to sleep close to their parents and many parents sleep better when their baby is near them.
- For a baby, falling asleep while feeding is natural and normal. Many parents intuitively let their baby feed himself to sleep.
- Bed sharing can help babies feel secure and sleep well. It also makes breastfeeding easier. But it needs to be done safely.
- Following your baby's natural sleeping pattern is likely to be easier on all of you than trying to impose a schedule.

8

Playing and learning

Just as your baby's body needs warmth, security and food, so her brain needs nourishment, too. She is like a sponge – constantly soaking up information and processing it, even when she's asleep. She is in learning mode 24/7. With your help, she will learn more in her first few years than in the whole of the rest of her life put together. Some of her learning will come from simply watching the world and taking it all in; some of it will happen as part of communicating and inter-acting with you and other people; but most of it will take place through experimentation and play.

Encouraging baby-led play means supporting your baby to have fun, learn and develop at her own pace. It means understanding her need for play, giving her the opportunity to play, and – as far as possible – allowing her to choose how to play, how long to play and what to play with. This chapter looks at what constitutes baby-led play and how it relates to learning, focusing on the period before your baby can crawl but with a look ahead to when she can get about by herself.

What is play?

Almost everything your baby does voluntarily is play. Playing encourages her to think and allows her to practise and perfect her physical skills. It stimulates her to reach out and roll over, and to want to learn about how things work. Babies are highly receptive – immersing themselves in learning, and absorbing information with all of their senses. They know what interests them and how to pace themselves, so that they can fully absorb each piece of information before moving on to something else. All they need is an environment in which their play can evolve freely and naturally.

When she's first born, most of your baby's learning is about relating to those close to her, forging attachments and adjusting to life outside the womb. The majority of her energy is spent coping with the huge changes in her body (having to breathe for herself and eat, for example) and on ensuring her survival. Her learning is done mainly from the safety of your arms, as she intently gathers information about the world immediately around her. The security she feels from being close to you night and day allows her to focus fully on taking in information, knowing she is safe. This will provide a foundation for learning throughout her life.

To your baby, everything is new. When she first discovers her hands, for example, she will spend many hours playing with them, finding out what they can do and, in the process, developing her dexterity. Her hands will be one of her main tools for play and learning, so she needs to understand how they work. Before she can handle toys and other objects she will be absorbed just by moving her wrists, opening and closing her fingers, and working out how to control the movement of her arms. Once she begins to be able to make her muscles do what she wants them to do, whole new possibilities for learning will suddenly open up. When, instead of simply looking at an interesting object, she finds she can reach out and touch it, pick it up, turn it over and move it, she'll begin to understand that she can make things happen – and she'll start to want to experiment on everything that comes within her reach.

Supporting your baby's play

Supporting your baby's play doesn't necessarily mean *helping* her to play. As adults, if we are absorbed in something, or busy learning a new skill – even if we get a bit frustrated – we don't usually want someone more capable to come along and do it for us. If they take over when we were just getting there, or if they misinterpret what we were trying to do and make something else happen instead, we can feel justifiably undermined, irritated and possibly even angry. It's the same for babies: having someone pre-guess their goal and intervene to 'help' them achieve it can be hugely frustrating for them and can often lead to tears. It can also get in the way of their learning and enjoyment.

> 'The simplest things keep her happy for ages. Taking a lid on and off a pot, putting something in a glass jar so she can watch it and rattle it – you can play like that anywhere – on a bus or a train, or at the dinner table. The whole world is a playground really. She's just fascinated by everything.'
>
> *Anthony, father of Lexi, 4 months*

Most of the time, babies are not actually trying to *achieve* anything when they play – it's the process that matters. It's the task itself that engages them, not the end product, and it's through *doing* that they learn. You may be itching to help your baby get all the shapes into the holes, but when she can't make the round piece fit through the square opening she is unlikely to have a sense of failure, just of discovery. She may be quite happy to have learnt that something doesn't work, without needing to find out (on this occasion) what does.

If your baby wants you to help or join in, she'll let you know. Mostly, she'll do this by taking her eyes off what she's playing with and looking at you instead. However, if she is constantly helped out *before* she signals that she's getting frustrated, she may learn to stop trying or thinking for herself. Being led by your baby means staying on the sidelines until she lets you know she needs you, or wants you to join in – and being ready to step back out again when she signals that she wants to take over – or when, as far as she's concerned, the task is completed.

While she's young, your baby will rely on you to provide things for her to play with but that doesn't mean you have to choose them for her. Offering her just two or three different things (babies can be overwhelmed by too much choice) will allow her to show you what interests her. If she's able to pick things up for herself, you can put a small selection within her reach and let her decide which one she wants to explore first. You may be surprised at what attracts her, or find it difficult to understand what she sees in something as simple as a wooden spoon. You can trust her, though – she knows what she's doing.

> 'I won't bother with baby classes this time. I've learnt you don't need to push babies – they get there in their own time. In hindsight, taking Thea to classes wasn't really to do with baby gym or music or whatever, it was about me making mummy friends. I don't need that this time – I've got lots of friends with kids now – I'll just let this one be.'
>
> *Sara, mother of Thea, 3 years, and expecting her second child*

Your baby is an athlete

Your baby's first toy – and probably the most important one for her to learn about – is her own body. From the moment she realises she can stretch out without coming up against the wall of the womb, she'll practise different movements in different combinations – gradually developing flexibility, balance, physical strength, co-ordination and mobility. Each

Baby walkers and bouncers can affect babies' development

Some babies enjoy spending time in swings, door bouncers and baby walkers. However, research suggests that, as well as posing safety risks (especially baby walkers), play equipment like this can encourage movements and postures for which the baby doesn't yet have the necessary balance or strength. The result can be that these aspects of her development don't have the chance to mature in the way they should (see page 14).

movement she makes is built on the last, and she'll progress to trying new things, instinctively, whenever she feels ready. All she needs is a bit of time and enough space to move in.

Many babies like to stay curled up for the first week or two, but after this they will usually enjoy spending time on a bed or the floor, discovering what their arms and legs can do and how to make their muscles work together. Even at two months, your baby will be able to change her position by wriggling and squirming, but she'll also be working on the strength and balance needed to roll over intentionally. Once this happens, you (and she) will find she can get across a room surprisingly quickly – although she may not always go in the direction she intended!

Once your baby has perfected getting on to her tummy by herself, she'll develop the co-ordination needed to crawl. This will be followed by her figuring out how to pull herself up on to her feet, and, eventually, how to walk. All she needs to develop these skills is the opportunity to practise – she is intent on becoming strong and mobile, and she knows instinctively what she needs to do. As long as you are close by, she'll let you know if she gets frustrated or stuck (for example, with an arm caught underneath her), but mostly she'll take care of herself.

Babies don't need tummy time

Parents are often told to put their baby on her tummy on the floor for a short period every day. This advice was introduced around the time of the back-to-sleep campaign, which followed the discovery that it was safer for babies to sleep on their backs. It was sparked by concerns that back-sleeping might not allow babies' neck and back muscles enough exercise and that their ability to roll over might be delayed as a result. Current research suggests that this worry was unfounded. However, a problem that had been relatively rare *is* now more common: when a baby spends a lot of time with her head pressed against something firm, such as a cot mattress, buggy or car seat, the back (or side) of her skull can become flattened. So 'tummy time' is now recommended to help prevent this.

Most young babies don't like tummy time – and it's not difficult to see why. When a baby is lying on her back on a flat surface she can move her arms and kick her legs in whatever combination and direction she wishes, and she can turn her head to the side easily to see a different view without needing to support its weight to do so. On her tummy, all of this is difficult, if not impossible. Moving one limb at a time just pushes her head and chest further into the floor. So, until she has the co-ordination to use both arms together, she is pretty much marooned. Even then, if she tries to reach out for a toy with one hand, she immediately falls flat again. It's frustrating for her.

Tummy time is a solution to a problem that exists only because we're a society whose babies spend a lot of time in cots, buggies and car seats, rather than being carried. When they're in an upright position in someone's arms or a sling, or lying on an adult's chest, there's no constant pressure on the back of the baby's head and their skull maintains a nice, rounded shape. They also use their neck and back muscles spontaneously when they're being held, to help them maintain their balance. So, if your baby spends most of her time in your arms she doesn't need to be made to lie on her tummy.

By the time she discovers how to get there by herself – at around five months – her muscles will be strong enough to make being in this position fun. In the meanwhile, there's no need to build tummy time into her day.

Babies often enjoy being able to move without the restriction of clothes and many prefer being undressed to being dressed, probably because of the sense of freedom that shedding their clothes brings. Many parents find that the time after a nappy change or before a bath is ideal for some clothes-free play. A thick towel will help protect the bed or carpet, and make the floor more comfortable; if the weather is warm enough, you and your baby could even go outside. Being naked will allow your baby to explore different parts of her body – especially the sensitive bits that are usually covered by a nappy. Until she's about six months old she won't be able to touch her feet by herself, so games like 'This little piggy' – where you wiggle each of her toes in turn – will be especially interesting. She may enjoy you kissing and blowing on her skin, naming her tummy, knees, ears and so on, or walking your fingers up and down, and you'll be helping her to learn how the various parts of her body are connected, at the same time. Don't be surprised if she seems very serious when you're playing with her like this; to her these are likely to be interesting sensations and discoveries and, while they may be enjoyable, they demand concentration.

Taking your baby swimming

A trip to the swimming pool will give your baby the opportunity to experience feelings of buoyancy and of moving her body in water. A swimming class will give you the company of other parents, and may help you feel more confident about handling your baby in the water, but there's no need to enrol in one unless you want to – your baby will give you plenty of clues as to how to help her enjoy the experience.

Babies get cold easily, so a toddler-and-baby pool, where the water is kept warmer than the main pool, will probably be more comfortable for her. You may also want to choose a quiet session to start with, until she is more confident – the sounds and smells of a swimming pool can be very scary the first few times. You can take your baby swimming from as young as six weeks, although some parents prefer to wait until after their baby's first lot of immunisations.

Your baby is a scientist

Babies see everything as a potential toy, demanding to be examined. They are intensely curious. They are interested in colour, size, weight, shape, texture and taste. They want to test things, to find out what they can do. This type of investigation begins quite young and gains momentum gradually. At about four months your baby will discover how to reach out and grasp objects on purpose, then, at around five months, she'll be able to bring them to her mouth with increasing accuracy. Once there, she will explore them intently. The nerve endings in her nose, lips and tongue are extremely sensitive and will give her an enormous amount of information about the object – what it tastes and smells like, whether it's hard or squishy, what the surface feels like, whether it's warm or cold, and so on. At around six months, she'll be able to twist and turn objects using both hands. This opens the way for her to subject them to a whole array of experiments – poking, squashing, waving, hitting, banging, chewing, dropping and throwing – just to see what happens.

Life, for a baby, is one long, exciting, self-taught physics lesson. Your baby may be too young to understand Newton's theory, but she is quite capable of discovering how gravity works, how some things bounce and others don't, how water finds its own level, how certain things sink while other things float and that big things don't fit in small holes. As adults, we take most of this for granted, without realising that we learned it through experimentation when we were very young. Your baby doesn't know what's going to happen when she tips up a cup or throws a toy – she needs to experiment to find out. And she'll need to do it again and again to truly understand about the angle and speed of tipping, the way different objects fall, and what breaks and what doesn't.

TV won't help your baby learn

Watching TV can keep babies amused for short periods but it doesn't really help them to learn because it's not interactive – even if what they are watching is designed to be educational. Babies learn mainly by doing or experiencing things for themselves – they need to be actively involved. Watching television is passive, and involves only sound and vision; your baby can't touch, hold, smell or taste the things she sees, and she can't control them or slow down the action. The people on the screen don't respond to her, either, if she tries to get their attention. So, while television may be a useful way to distract her occasionally, if you need a break, in general she'll learn more when she's not watching TV.

'Babies look really intently at things so I can usually tell what Isla is interested in. If it's out of her reach, I'll take her closer, or bring it to her and we'll look at it together. It can be something as simple as the leaves on a tree moving in the wind or a piece of shiny paper. If it's something she can hold or touch, she'll usually spend ages with it – as though that piece of shiny paper is the most amazing, precious thing she's ever seen. You just have to be really quiet and let her take her time. You can see she's concentrating hard, taking it all in. I love watching her.'

Mark, father of Isla, 5 months

Your baby is an explorer

Babies instinctively indulge in what's called 'seeking behaviour'. Their natural curiosity drives them to explore their surroundings – and everything within reach. Once your baby can crawl or walk, the opportunities available to her for discovering new places and unearthing new things to experiment on will expand rapidly, but until then, she'll be relying on you to bring things she wants to touch or smell within her reach. Babies use all of their senses to learn, and the more varied the experiences you can offer her, the greater will be her learning. There's no need to go out of your way, though – your everyday surroundings are likely to be a rich source of things that will interest your baby. From her point of view almost everything is new and worthy of her attention. Here are some ideas for things she might enjoy exploring with each of her senses:

- **Smell**: Offer her things to hold and she'll inevitably sniff them – flowers, soap, food (especially foods with interesting smells, such as lemons, cinnamon sticks or strong cheese).
- **Taste**: As soon as your baby can get things to her mouth she will explore them with her lips and tongue. (Make sure nothing she can get hold of is poisonous, or likely to be a choking hazard.)
- **Sound**: Listen together to birds singing, the wind in the trees, music, people laughing. She'll probably enjoy toys

or objects that make a noise too, such as rattles, shakers or bells, though she may find it easier to focus on one sound at a time.

- **Touch**: Babies are fascinated by different textures. Anything from pebbles and pumice stones to different fabrics, sand and water. Food can be interesting to touch, too – for example, a piece of broccoli or a lump of pastry dough. Your baby may also enjoy experiencing different sensations on her skin, such as being stroked gently with a feather.

- **Sight**: Anything around your baby can act as a stimulus, from patterns and shapes to animals, buildings and objects. Newborn babies tend to prefer stark contrasts of dark and light but they quickly learn to pick out finer detail and subtle colours.

'I realised after a while that it's better to be outside every day than worry about surrounding the baby with books and toys at home. They learn so much more outside.'

Elizabeth, mother of Alessandra, 11 months

Playing with your baby

You are your baby's first and – until she is old enough to make friends – her best playmate. While she is very young she will be completely reliant on you to provide her with an opportunity to play. Before she is able to grab things for herself, she'll need you to offer them to her, so that she can look at them and touch them. Later, a great deal of her play will be experimenting with things by herself, with you available nearby to help if she needs you. But she will enjoy learning *with* you, too.

In the early months, your baby will want to be in contact with you most of the time, so the activities she enjoys will tend to be limited to face-to-face interactions, such as imitating your expressions, poking her tongue out, and being talked and sung to, and rocked in your arms. But from about three months onwards she will begin to be slightly more adventurous. She may like:

- being bounced gently on your knee in time to songs and rhymes
- having her fingers and toes played with
- being held in your arms while you dance
- being swung gently (in a cradle hold)

From around four months, when she is beginning to get a sense of herself as an individual, separate from you, and to understand that things exist even when she can't see them, she will start to enjoy:

- looking at her reflection (and yours) in a mirror
- games with an element of tension or surprise, such as peek-a-boo or 'round and round the garden' (although you'll need to be sensitive to the level of surprise she can cope with)
- being lifted high in the air and then swooped low
- having 'raspberries' blown on her tummy
- clapping games

It's important to be alert to your baby's signals that she wants to play – or that she doesn't want to. Sometimes adults try to engage a baby in play without realising that she may be studying something that's caught her interest, or dealing with information overload (see page 83). Letting your baby lead the way will help to keep her play fun, absorbing and at a level she is comfortable with. It will also help her to develop a sense of give and take; accepting things when she offers them to you, showing your delight and giving them back, will let her know that her gestures are valued, and that she can expect the same from other people.

Even quite young babies enjoy looking at books with an adult for short periods. When your baby is newborn, she will probably prefer very simple, black and white images but she'll soon show an interest in colours and more complex pictures. Linking the images to real life, for example by pointing at a picture of a dog, talking about the sound it makes and relating this (either at the time or later) to your own dog, or to one you see in the park, will help your baby to grasp that squiggles on a page can represent actual things. This is the very beginning of helping her to want to make her own drawings and learn to read and write.

Babies can't share

Once they reach about six months of age, babies become interested in other children, and will be happy to play alongside them. However, a baby of this age has no understanding of making friends or how to play together; taking turns and sharing will be beyond her capability for at least another couple of years. She won't be able to join in the games of her siblings, either (and they may need help to understand this). Trying to persuade your baby to share her toys or her space (or you!), or to respect the belongings and activities of other people, before she is able to understand, is likely to make her confused or frustrated. She'll begin to do all of this spontaneously when she is ready, as her awareness of other people's feelings grows.

The fun, excitement and pleasure you and your baby share through simple games of singing, clapping, pulling funny faces and making silly noises creates a foundation for friendship, language and social skills. It's not only a great way to spend time together but it will set her on the path to easy interaction with adults, and to sharing and playing with other children later.

Toys and other playthings

Many parents find that small children and babies seem to get the most play value from very simple things. For example, an empty yoghurt pot can be fascinating for a young baby – and the packaging from a new toy often proves to have far more scope for play and exploration than the toy itself, for children of all ages. Babies want to copy, too, so they naturally want to play with whatever those around them are handling. Everyday functional objects or materials from nature can offer your baby just as much stimulation and opportunity to learn as purpose-made toys – not least because they will teach her about the real world, which is what she most wants to understand. Anything that isn't potentially harmful (for example, sharp, poisonous or a choking hazard), and is robust – or safe and easy to replace if it does get broken – can be a toy.

As your baby gets older, toys and objects that she can explore fully and do things *with* or *to* without risk of harm are likely to have more play and learning value than toys that entertain her, but over which she has no real control. They don't have to be made especially for babies – they can be from your kitchen cupboard – but it's worth bearing in mind that at some point everything will find its way to your baby's mouth, so you may want to avoid non-baby-safe plastics and other potentially harmful materials. Cups and bowls, wooden blocks, empty boxes and pegs offer lots of potential for stimulating play and real-world learning.

'The best thing anybody ever bought us for the baby was a cheap set of plastic stacking cups. They've been used almost every day since he was about five months – for sorting, building, collecting things, pouring water in the bath. He loves them.'

Ellie, mother of Austin, 2 years

Learning through messy play

Materials such as water, sand, mud and clay act like a magnet for older babies, and playing with them offers lots of opportunities for scientific discovery and creativity. It enables them to learn how to pour, measure and mix, to understand weight and volume, and to experiment with changing shapes. But enjoyment of 'messy play' begins very early – even as a newborn, your baby will be interested in watching and feeling water being poured and splashed while in the bath. By the time she's four or five months she'll probably enjoy being held near the sink to splash in a bowl of water or to play with bubbles, and from about six months she will be ready to start discovering what jugs, cups, straws, spoons, funnels and sieves can do.

The opportunity to handle food (see page 120) will open up a wealth of tactile experiences for your baby, as well as allowing her to discover different tastes. Letting her watch (and 'help') while you cook will be a great way for her to learn about colours, textures and flavours – and, later, about cutting, measuring and mixing. Meanwhile, playing with pastry or bread dough and sauces will give her a chance to experiment with squishing and spreading without risk of coming to harm if she puts her fingers in her mouth.

Far from encouraging children to make a mess at other times, messy play actually allows them to learn how to avoid mess. For example, practice at pouring in the bath makes it less likely that your baby will spill the water she is offered in an open cup at the table, while using a small spade or a spoon to shovel sand will help her develop the skills she will need to use cutlery.

'One of the most useful pieces of advice I was ever given about bringing up kids was to stop and ask myself, "Do I really have to say no?" It's so easy to say it without even thinking, when, actually, maybe it *is* okay to stick your fingers in the jam or splash in a puddle.'

Agata, mother of Piotr, 4, Jedrek, 2 years, and Ewelina, 7 months

Your baby may be wary, at first, of new playthings and look to you for confirmation that they're safe. This is particularly likely in the case of messy materials. She will take your expression and what you say very seriously. For example, if you pull a face or say, 'Ugh!' when handling something sticky, she may be hesitant about having a go with anything that looks similar, whereas a reassuring look will encourage her to investigate. Babies sometimes need a little time before they are ready to touch new things – many are wary of sand, for instance, the first time they encounter it. If your baby sees you handling an unfamiliar texture, she's more likely to decide to copy you. If she doesn't, it doesn't matter – there's no hurry. She will have absorbed some information about it and may be ready to touch another time.

Dressing for mess

Whenever your baby is enjoying messy play, it's fair to assume she will get herself and her surroundings wet or dirty – or both. If you're prepared for this, you'll be more relaxed about letting her enjoy her experiments. Dress her in something that won't bother you if it gets stained or, if it's warm enough, let her play with no clothes on, or in just a nappy. Failing that, a long-sleeved bib or hand-me-down top, and a plastic sheet on the floor, will help contain the mess.

Balancing learning with safety

Whether at home or outside, your little athlete, scientist and budding explorer needs to be able to play in safety. This doesn't mean overprotecting her, but it does mean taking some basic precautions. To her, her surroundings are there to be explored, examined and tested. She will conduct her investigations without any awareness of what an object is supposed to be used for, how precious, dangerous or breakable it is, how much mess might be created, or how frustrating or time-consuming the consequences might be for you. She is on a mission to learn, and she'll pursue this purposefully and instinctively. She's also driven by the need to fit into the world she finds herself in; she wants to understand what is expected of her, and how she is supposed to behave, and she looks to you to help her. However, her level of understanding means that she isn't able to make connections between events, or to figure out what she is and isn't allowed to do.

Your baby will naturally want to:

- **Touch interesting things.** This includes anything she can reach, even if (you know) it's fragile, dangerous or valuable. She will want to push, poke and prod, just to see what happens.
- **Copy those around her.** This means that, if she sees you using a remote control or mobile phone, or drinking a glass of wine, she will want to have a go as well.
- **Develop and practise her physical skills.** For a younger baby this could mean grasping your necklace or hair; for an older baby it might be grabbing at your food or pulling things off shelves.

Some of her actions, such as pulling someone's hair, may be undesirable; others, such as knocking over a cup of tea, may even be unsafe – but your baby doesn't know this. She isn't being naughty – she has no idea that what she does may sometimes be inconvenient, irritating or embarrassing. If you tell her off she won't learn anything about why you didn't want her to do what she did – and she won't understand why you suddenly seem to be annoyed. Being aware of what she might be able to reach will mean you can keep precious or dangerous things safely out of her way. And if she's doing something you'd rather she didn't do, you'll probably find that distraction is more effective than trying to teach her 'no'.

Many parents say that the first time their baby rolled over they couldn't believe how far she managed to move in how short a time. Overnight – and well before your baby can crawl – electric wires, trailing cords and doors that could trap fingers can begin to present a risk. Keeping your growing explorer safe will be easier if you acknowledge just how irresistible everything is to her, and how much practice she needs to develop and consolidate her skills. Taking some time to see your house from her perspective will enable you to make some adjustments in advance. A few minutes spent crawling around will quickly reveal what your baby may soon be able to reach from the floor. Look at everything you come across and ask yourself whether it could harm her. If it could, either move it up (dangling curtain cords) or lock it up (bleach). If it's not likely to be harmful, ask yourself if it could be easily damaged (or spilt) – and whether that would matter. If the answer to both these questions is 'yes', then simply move it to somewhere she can't reach.

At about the same time that your baby is developing the skills that will enable her to move around, she will also be discovering how to use her fingers to open boxes, tins and bottles, insert things into slots and press switches. Rather than lock everything away, you may prefer to change round some of your cupboards so that things that can take a bit of bashing are available for her to explore. For instance, you could decide to keep saucepans and plastic food containers in a low cupboard, where she can sit and play with them while you're washing up or preparing a meal.

> 'I offered Lilly-Rose a new toy to play with the other day and I was surprised how much she seemed to get out of it. I just thought: "Why didn't I let her have a go with it before?" It's like she's one step ahead of me all the time. I just get used to her being able to do one thing and then she's on to the next thing. I'm constantly trying to keep up.'
>
> *Tessa, mother of Lilly-Rose, 11 months*

As she gets older, your baby will become more interested in looking at and touching things outside the house – and she'll probably want to test them in her mouth, too. Worms, snails, flowers, leaves and stones are all potentially fascinating to a young child, but dog poo, broken glass and ants' nests may be equally interesting. You may find it useful to have something really exciting to distract your baby with, in case she is desperate to explore something potentially harmful when you're playing outside with her.

It's also important to trust her to take small risks. Babies need to be allowed to decide what they feel capable of and to try new things – otherwise the urge to have a go can become so strong that it overrides their judgement. Seeing the world from your baby's point of view, and trusting her to know her limitations, will help you to share her excitement *and* ensure she stays safe.

Spontaneous, baby-led play can happen anytime, anywhere, helping your baby to enjoy exploration and learning. Supporting her to test out her environment and explore the world means finding a balance that allows her to try new things and develop new skills, while at the same time keeping her (and everything around her!) safe. The closer and more responsive you are in all areas of her life, the more easily you'll be able to understand her behaviour and anticipate it, so that learning is as enjoyable and stress-free as possible. That way she'll continue to be curious and want to learn about the world as she moves into toddlerhood and beyond.

Key points

- To your baby, playing and learning are the same thing.
- Most babies like company while they play but they need to play at their own pace; too much help can disrupt their learning.
- Babies are naturally curious – they have an inbuilt need to investigate everything around them.
- Babies don't need complex or expensive toys – everyday items can be just as interesting to them.
- Learning sometimes involves mess. Being prepared for it, and sharing your child's sense of discovery, will make it easier to cope with.
- Babies use their senses to learn; offering your baby a variety of experiences – both indoor and outdoor – will give her lots of opportunity for discovery and fun.
- Thinking ahead about safety issues can make playtimes more relaxed.

9

Caring for your baby, day by day

Looking after your baby will include lots of small tasks, many of which, on the surface, may appear quite mundane. Some will be repeated over and over, every day. But babies enjoy repetition, and day-to-day activities can be fun for them. The secret is to do things *with* your baby rather than *to* him, so that he shares what is happening rather than simply having to tolerate it. Seeing everyday baby-care activities through your baby's eyes, acknowledging how he may feel, and allowing yourself to be guided by him, will help to make the most ordinary things – such as washing and dressing him, changing nappies and going out – enjoyable for both of you.

Your baby can also be involved in decision-making, if you let him. There will inevitably be lots of choices you have to make on his behalf, but if you stop to ask yourself each time whether it's possible for *him* to be the one to choose you'll probably find there are plenty of occasions when he can have a say, too. This chapter suggests some ways to make the most of the little things you and your baby do together every day.

Dealing with wees and poos

In terms of our history, using nappies to keep wees and poos contained is a relatively modern practice, and many babies

181

aren't great fans of it. Human babies, like all animals, are primed not to soil themselves. Some don't seem to mind being in a dirty or very wet nappy but others will protest loudly. Most don't really enjoy having their nappy changed, especially when they're very young. Being alert for signs that your baby is about to – or has just done a – wee or poo, and finding ways to make nappy changing less stressful, can help to make this aspect of parenting as pleasant as possible for both of you.

Most babies prefer to be without a nappy. It's healthier, too, for them to have at least some nappy-free time, to lessen the chances of nappy rash. It's also a good way for parents to learn the signs that indicate their baby needs to 'go', so that they can minimise the number of dirty nappies they have to deal with – or even do without them altogether (see page 185).

The majority of Western parents use nappies most of the time; but whether you use them all the time, occasionally or not at all, getting to know the signs that your baby needs to wee or poo will help you and him to stay in touch with his body's rhythms. Eventually, he will learn how to tell you in words that a poo or wee is coming; in the meantime, encouraging him to recognise the signals that let him know what's happening means he won't be faced with having to learn this all over again in a few years' time, when you really *do* want to avoid dirty nappies. A baby-led approach from the start can make learning to use the potty or toilet something that happens gradually and effortlessly, as a natural part of growing up.

Getting to know the signs

The signs that a wee or poo is imminent can be very subtle and will be easiest to detect if you're in close contact with your baby. You'll probably pick up the poo-coming signs quite quickly but, at first, you may not register a wee until it's actually happening.

Before a poo your baby may:

- grimace
- squirm
- stare blankly
- grunt
- cry suddenly
- pause in the middle of feeding

Many parents report that their baby also makes his own unique facial expression, which only they recognise – and most people can tell when a baby goes red in the face that he is actually doing a poo!

Before a wee your baby may just squirm or wriggle slightly, or you may simply feel him tighten his thigh muscles. But even before you are able to recognise these clues, you may have already begun to notice that he tends to wee a predictable length of time after he's fed or woken up. From there, it's a short step to reading the signs that it's about to happen.

Nappy changing

Your baby's nappy is likely to need changing at least six times a day. Whether you use disposables, pre-formed all-in-one reusables or even old-style fold-it-yourself terry nappies, thinking about nappy changing from your baby's point of view can provide some useful hints for how to make it a pleasant experience. You'll soon work out which of the following suggestions work for you and your baby:

- Talk to your baby about what's happening: let him know that you're going to change his nappy because he's done a poo (or wee), and explain what you are doing as you do it. (Some parents start by asking their baby if he'd like his nappy changed.)

- Consider whether your baby may prefer to have his nappy changed on the floor or a bed rather than a changing table, so that he can roll from side to side and move his arms and legs comfortably – or, especially while he's tiny, whether he might be happier on your lap.
- If your baby doesn't like being undressed, put him in clothes that are easy to undo from the bottom (see page 192), so you don't have to strip him off completely. (Modern versions of baby gowns – sometimes known as bundlers – can be especially handy for newborns.)
- If the changing surface is plastic your baby may prefer to lie on a warm towel or cloth nappy, or a thick layer of kitchen paper.
- Babies often wee as soon as they are on the changing mat – a muslin over a little boy's front, and a baby girl's clothes pushed well out of the way, should help to prevent everyone getting a soaking.
- If your baby's poo has made its way up his back or down his legs, he may find being washed in a shallow bath of warm water, or using a warm shower (after getting the worst off with a soft tissue or cloth) more comfortable than lots of wiping.
- If you are using disposable 'wet wipes' try one on your own chest first, to see how it feels – some can be very cold on unsuspecting skin. Many babies prefer the feel of warm water, on cotton wool or a flannel.
- Your baby may enjoy a game incorporated into the nappy changing, like 'This little piggy', or having 'raspberries' blown on his tummy.

Some parents find that getting their baby to help with nappy changing means they don't have to pull him about quite so much; it's also a way of helping him to feel that he is actively taking part. Experiment by pressing gently on your baby's leg and asking him to move it. If you give him time to register the sensation, he'll respond by moving it in that direction. If you say the same little phrase each time, he'll gradually begin to respond to the words alone.

> 'I always change Sara on the floor. It's her world and she feels safe – and she can't fall off anything. And I always tell her what I'm doing and what's going to happen next. It means she's always been relaxed about nappy changing – there are no surprises. It's such a lovely, intimate time together.'
>
> *Cath, mother of Sara, 9 months*

No nappies

Not using any nappies at all is common practice in many traditional societies, where mothers carry their babies almost constantly and quickly learn the signs (or develop a sense) of when their child needs to wee or poo. This is becoming increasingly popular – at least as a partial approach – in the UK, where it is usually known as 'natural infant hygiene' or 'elimination communication' (EC – see 'Sources of Information and Support', page 227). It's *not* the same as attempting to train your baby to use a potty, or expecting him to have control over his bowel or bladder muscles before he is really able to. It's simply learning his signals or typical timings and responding to them by holding him – usually with his legs in a squatting position – over a potty or toilet (or, if you are outside, a suitable patch of ground). Some parents use a sound cue each time their baby goes (a 'pssss' sound is common for wees in many cultures), which the baby learns to associate with relaxing the appropriate muscles.

Some parents using this approach start watching for their baby's elimination signs from birth and begin catching wees straight away; others wait until they feel more confident – perhaps when the intensity of the first few months is over. Most do a flexible version of no nappies – for example, using them when they are out and about or visiting relatives, and leaving the baby nappy-free at home. If you do decide to do without nappies some or all of the time, expect lots of misses as well as catches – it will be a year or two before he's able to tell you reliably when he needs to go.

> 'I hardly ever use nappies with Rosy. If I'm holding her or she's in the sling she'll just wriggle until she's held somewhere she can wee – she'll never wee in bed or when I'm holding her close. She lets me know when she needs to go.'
>
> *Susy, mother of Jack, 6, Grace, 4 years, and Rosy, 17 months*

Washing and bathing

Some babies love bath time; others, especially when they are very young, can find it an uncomfortable – or even frightening – experience. Trying to manage a wet, slippery and unhappy baby in a baby bath can also be stressful for parents. However, most young babies don't need to be bathed very often. Newborns often don't need a bath at all for the first week or so, and delaying their first full wash gives the covering of natural moisturiser they are born with – known as vernix – a chance to be absorbed into their skin. Even when your baby is crawling and eating solid food, he's unlikely to need a bath every day. The only really important bits to keep clean and dry are the places that could get sore, such as the face, skin creases (for example, the armpits) and nappy area, and his hands and forearms, which he's likely to suck.

On the other hand, bathing isn't only about getting clean – it can be both fun and relaxing. A bath is a great opportunity to help your baby learn about his body, too. If you can make it something your baby enjoys, bathing can happen whenever you and he like, and last as long as you both want.

Massage is good for babies

Touch is one of your baby's most fundamental needs, and most babies love to be massaged. It's good for their skin, nervous system, circulation and digestion, as well as being both soothing and stimulating. It can also help them to sleep. All babies can benefit, but massage is especially good for babies with special needs and those who were born early – they have been found to grow better and have healthier bones than non-massaged babies.

There is no right or wrong way to massage your baby; if you follow his lead – repeating what he likes and avoiding what he doesn't like – you won't go far wrong. You may want to join a local baby massage group, to give you more confidence and to meet other parents, but here are some ideas, to help you get started:

- Make sure your baby isn't hungry, the room is warm and you won't be disturbed.
- Undress your baby and lay him on a firm, soft surface, such as a folded (or thick) towel on the floor (a plastic changing mat will feel cold and may get too slippery).
- Use a simple, non-perfumed oil (avoid mustard and nut oils, which can cause irritation). Pour the oil into your dry hands and warm it between your palms – putting cold oil straight on to your baby could make him jump.
- Start with firm strokes, mostly downwards and outwards from the centre of his body. Massage with your whole hand and with your fingertips; experiment with circular movements and different degrees of pressure (not too hard!), to find out what he likes. Aim to cover his whole body in the course of the massage – including individual fingers and toes.
- Keep one hand or finger on your baby's body at all times, so that there is constant contact between you. Lifting your hands on and off breaks the soothing rhythm.

- Watch, listen and feel for his reactions and adapt what you're doing in response to his signals, especially if he seems to have had enough. Some babies enjoy being talked to during a massage; others prefer singing, humming or quiet.
- When you're ready to finish, hold one or both hands still against your baby's tummy or back for a few seconds, as a sign that the massage is over and you are going to take your hands away.

Of course, you can use stroking movements to soothe or communicate with your baby whenever you like, but time set aside for a massage will be particularly rewarding for both of you. Massage shuts off the production of stress hormones and stimulates the release of the hormones that help with bonding. It's an ideal way for you to get to know your baby and to comfort and calm both of you.

Caring for your baby's skin

Too much washing can quickly cause a baby's skin to become dry – especially if soaps and body washes are used. Products aimed at adults and older children are almost always unsuitable, because they tend to be either too harsh or highly perfumed (or both), but even baby products can be drying. Babies don't need shampoo, either, unless their hair is really dirty. Some disposable wipes can cause irritation, so it's a good idea to test a new brand on a small (non-sensitive) area of your baby's bottom several hours before you start to use it. An occasional all-over massage with a suitable oil (see above) will help to make sure your baby's skin stays soft.

Sharing a bath can be fun

While it's fine to use a baby bath – or a deep bowl or bucket, or even the kitchen sink – to bath your baby in, many young babies dislike being bathed this way. Most feel safer when taken into their parent's bath. Sharing your bath with your baby has lots of benefits:

- You can both relax – together.
- You can hold your baby more securely than you can when he's in a baby bath.
- It's an extra opportunity for some skin-to-skin time.
- The water stays warm for longer in a big bath (and you can tell more easily if your baby is getting cold, and alter the water temperature accordingly).
- You can use both hands to give your baby an all-over wash or massage.
- Washing your baby's hair is easier with him laid back against your thighs than it is with him in a baby bath (or held over a sink), and more comfortable for him.
- A mother–baby bath enables easy breastfeeding. In fact, sharing a bath with your baby can be helpful in sorting out some common breastfeeding problems, such as difficulties with latching on, and breast refusal.

In order to enjoy a shared bath safely and easily it's best to have someone else's help. That way they can undress your baby and pass him to you once you are in the water, and you can pass him back to them later to be dried (giving you the chance to use grown-up bath products and have an extended soak). If no one is available to help, experiment with a low table or Moses basket alongside the bath, so you can lift your baby in and out easily without slipping. You may find doing things in the following order helpful:

- Once you are undressed, undress your baby, wrap him in a towel and place him where he will be safe, next to the bath (you may need to keep one hand on him in case he rolls).
- Get in the bath yourself, then unwrap your baby and lift him in on top of you.
- When you're finished, lift your baby out on to his towel and wrap him up in it while you get out. Dress him quickly, so he doesn't get cold.

Once he is able to sit up without support your baby may well be happy in the big bath by himself – and it's an ideal place for him to learn about pouring and measuring, with cups, funnels and sieves. But he'll probably continue to enjoy the option of a shared bath for several more years.

'My first baby hated bath time – it was always a bit of a struggle with the baby bath. With my second I felt so much more confident. I just brought her into my bath and used my common sense about how hot to have it – she'd have let me know if it was too hot or cold. She loves it – and you can just see she's learning so much.'

Juana, mother of Emilia, 5 years, and Daniela, 11 months

Tips for enjoyable baths – whether shared or solo

However you bath your baby, there are lots of ways to make sure the experience is enjoyable and comfortable for him. Here are some ideas:

- **Keep your baby warm.** Babies catch cold quickly, especially when they're wet. Make sure the room is warm, with no draughts, before you start, and keep the bath water at around 37°C/99°F (blood temperature) or slightly warmer – it should feel pleasantly warm on the inside of your wrist. Keeping most of your baby's body under the water, or laying a flannel over his back or chest, will help him to stay warm.

- **Notice his reactions.** Lower him into the water gently, so he has a chance to register what is happening. Find out what he enjoys – he may want you to talk to him, play with him or sing to him. He might like to splash or he may prefer gentle swishing, or to have water poured over him. If he isn't enjoying the bath, and you aren't able to reassure him, take him out.
- **Help him to stay relaxed afterwards,** with a cuddle, a massage (see page 187) or a feed.

Dressing and undressing

Battles over getting dressed and undressed are common, especially when babies are old enough to resist what their parent is trying to do. This sort of struggle can be avoided or eased by taking time to make getting dressed an enjoyable experience that your baby can participate in. Allowing him to make choices from early on will help him to feel he has some say in getting dressed. Even young babies can show by reaching out that they like the colour or texture of a particular item of clothing. (They can be overwhelmed by too many alternatives, though, so it's best to limit the options to two or three things.) If you have to insist on something – a hat in the winter, for example – being allowed to choose *which* hat may make wearing one more acceptable to him. Some parents also find their baby is more likely to be happy to wear something when he can watch in the mirror as it's being put on. Talking to your baby about being too hot or cold, especially while you're dressing and undressing him, will help him begin to understand the connection between clothes and comfort.

If your baby seems unhappy and you can't work out why, check his clothes aren't causing a problem. Shoulder straps that fall down, and stiff materials such as denim, can restrict babies' movements and frustrate them, while thick snowsuits can make bending elbows and knees almost impossible. Waistbands can dig into a baby's tummy and be painful, and Velcro is often scratchy. Check inside socks and tights, and the feet of babygrows, for hanging threads that could wrap themselves around your baby's toes and restrict the blood supply.

Caring for your baby's feet

Going barefoot is better for our feet than wearing shoes – and even more so for babies, whether or not they can walk. So if it's warm enough, bare feet are best for your baby. Toes can also be squashed (and the soft bones damaged) by socks and all-in-ones that are too tight. If your baby's toes reach the end of a babygrow when he stretches out his leg, the suit is starting to be too small. If the rest of it is still quite roomy, and you want him to go on wearing it, cut off the feet and, if it's cold, put socks or bootees on him instead.

Putting things on and taking them off

It will sometimes feel as though you are getting your baby in and out of clothes all day. Choosing clothes that are quick and easy to manage will make dressing and undressing more comfortable for him and save time and frustration for both of you. For example, neckbands that open with poppers (press studs) or buttons mean you don't have to squeeze your baby's head through a tight hole – something lots of babies find stressful. Similarly, a babygrow with poppers that extend well below the knee on at least one leg means a lot less pulling about during dressing and nappy changing.

How clothes are put on or taken off can make a big difference to how enjoyable the procedure is for babies. Here are some tips – you and your baby may find lots more:

- As with nappy changing, telling him what you are doing and giving him the chance to join in, for example, by asking him to lift his arm (and giving him time to respond), will help him feel he is taking part in the process – even if it takes a while for him to understand what you are saying.
- If jumpers and T-shirts don't open widely at the neck, putting them on over the crown of your baby's head first, then pulling them down over his face, will allow the neck hole to pass over the narrowest part of his head while also protecting his throat. When removing it, lifting the jumper upwards over your baby's face first will be more comfortable for him, as well as minimising the amount of time his face is covered.
- Sleeves can be tricky, and little fingers are vulnerable. Until he gets the hang of it and is able to help, explain to your baby that you need to lift or bend his arm; then put your fingers or hand into the sleeve from the bottom, engulf his hand and pull it through gently. There is less risk this way that his fingers will be bent back. Do the same thing with his feet for tight trousers or leggings.
- For all-in-one babygrows and suits, experiment with putting your baby's legs in first – especially if the opening doesn't extend past his knees. Bending his legs high enough to get them in after his arms are in the sleeves is likely to be quite difficult for you – and uncomfortable for him.

Avoiding overheating

When the weather's cold, keeping your baby warm will be your priority, but it's important to be aware that babies are just as prone to overheating, if overwrapped, as they are at risk of getting too cold. Many shops and cafes are surprisingly hot in the winter and your baby will quickly begin to suffer if he's in a thick snowsuit. The same is true in cars, trains and buses – once the heating gets going, these places can be just as warm as the inside of your house.

A very young baby isn't always able to let his parents know he's uncomfortable; he may just go into a deep sleep, getting hotter all the while. An older baby, on the other hand, may react by struggling and crying, which can easily be interpreted as an objection to being held, or strapped into a buggy, rather than a sign that something else is wrong. Just unzipping your baby's coat or suit and removing his hood or hat will help to prevent him getting too hot. Some babies also begin to associate layers of clothes with discomfort, and can become resistant to having outdoor clothes put on. For a baby who isn't likely to move around much, a thick blanket or shawl that can be opened easily may be a better option for trips outside than a thick coat or snowsuit.

Some parents find they can avoid the risks of overheating and the hassle of dressing their baby in extra layers when they go out by leaving him in his indoor clothes and carrying him in a sling. With a big coat wrapped around both of them, the parent's body will keep the baby warm – and they'll be close enough to sense if he's getting too hot.

Getting around with your baby

Parents use a variety of equipment for getting out and about with their baby, whether on foot or by car, carrying him or pushing him, depending on their baby's needs and preferences and the practicalities of each situation. The most common are slings, buggies and car seats.

Using a sling

Many parents find that the most practical way of getting around with their baby is to carry him in a sling. It allows them to have their hands free, while keeping their little one safe and warm. A sling can make shopping, using public transport, or going anywhere that is crowded or has steps, easier to manage than using a buggy.

Many babies much prefer being in a sling to being strapped into a seat. This is understandable: young babies can find busy and noisy places scary – being carried in a sling is reassuring and means they can get their parent's attention easily when they need something. Older babies want to be on the move and able to explore, and they don't like being constrained for long periods. Being close to you in a sling for

You can 'wear' your baby indoors, too

Carrying your baby in a sling around the house has lots of benefits, especially in the early weeks and months. Here are just a few:

- You can comfort him or rock him to sleep without really having to do anything.
- You get the very earliest signs that he needs something.
- It helps you tune in to his movements and murmurs.
- You always know where he is, and that he's safe (not being poked by your toddler or sat on by the cat!)
- If you need to pop out in a hurry, you can just grab *your* coat (to wrap around both of you) and dash out of the door.

some of the time may make being in a fixed seat, when he has to be, more acceptable for your baby.

'The first time I went out with Cecilie in her brand new buggy I felt like a "proper" mum. But she seemed a million miles away from me and I wanted her to be close – I was sure that's what she needed. So I just left the buggy at home after that. I'd go out with her in the sling and have a little bag with a couple of nappies and wipes. It was all we needed – it was great.'

Martina, mother of Cecilie, 2 years

Slings come in a variety of styles: ring sling, wrap sling, Mei Tai, pouch and soft structured carrier. Some are designed to be worn in only one or two ways; others can be worn on the adult's front, back or hip, with the baby either upright or cradled. The most versatile have a do-it-yourself wrap-around design that can be tied differently, according to the age of the baby. A sling that supports your baby against you in a cradled position is likely to be particularly useful in the early weeks, especially if you're breastfeeding. If you opt for an upright carrier, choose one that supports your baby in a squatting (or 'froggy') position, with his thighs apart and his knees bent (and higher than his bottom) – this is thought to be a safer position for a baby's hips than with his legs dangling vertically from his crotch.

A sling should always be worn so that your baby is held tightly against you, supporting his back and helping to keep his airway clear (loose, bag-style pouches are *not* safe, especially for babies under about five months, who cannot hold their head and trunk upright). To support his back and neck – and protect yours – wear your baby hitched high up on your chest (or, when he's older, your back), rather than at waist level. You should be able to kiss the top of his head easily. This position also means you can see his face and know that he is safe, and it will help to keep his chin away from his chest, so that he can breathe easily. This is especially important if he falls asleep, as he is very likely to do. The box below provides a useful checklist for when your baby hitches a ride with you.

Keeping your little HITCHhiker safe

To be sure you and your baby are both comfortable and safe when you're carrying him in a sling on your front make sure he is well **HITCH**ed:

- **H**igh enough for you to kiss the top of his head easily
- **I**n view at all times
- **T**ight against you
- **C**hin off (his) chest
- **H**ips open and knees bent, in a 'froggy' position (if in an upright sling)

Once your baby can support his neck and head well, you'll be able to carry him on your back. He'll still need to be **H**igh – and with open **H**ips, in a structured carrier – and **T**ight too, if it's a soft sling – even though you won't be able to see him or kiss him.

Some slings allow parents to carry their baby facing outwards. However, when your baby is very young he's likely to get quickly overstimulated when looking out at the world, and he won't be able to snuggle into you when he's had enough. An outward-facing position will also prevent his spine from following its natural curve. Once he is able to sit up without support this will be less important but, by then, you may find that a sling worn on your hip or back is easier.

Many parents of twins say that a sling is indispensable if you have more than one baby. It's possible to carry two small babies in some types of sling, but the real benefit comes from being able to put a happy or sleeping baby in the sling and have two hands free to soothe a grumpy baby, or for two parents to carry a baby each. If you are going out on your own, wearing one baby and pushing the other means you can get away with a single buggy, which is likely to be more manoeuvrable than a double one. If you have a toddler as well, taking a sling and a double buggy means your older child will also be able to ride or sleep if she needs to.

Some parents manage to wear two slings at the same time, either for twins or for a baby and a toddler. The slings don't have to be the same design – in fact it may help if they're not. You can wear one baby on your front and one on your back, or carry them one on each hip. The important thing is to ensure appropriate support for both babies and an even distribution of weight to protect your back. You may need to experiment a few times to find out which sling (or baby) to put on first.

If possible, try out a variety of slings before you decide which style(s) will work best for you. Some parent–baby groups hold sling workshops where you can discuss the merits of the various styles with parents who've used them, and there's lots of information online, too (see 'Sources of Information and Support', page 228). If you want to keep your options open and be ready in case your needs change – or if you and your partner prefer different styles – you may want to buy (or borrow) more than one type of sling.

'I often used to carry Anna in a sling so she could hear me, see me and smell me – while I got on with what needed doing. I'd do most of the cooking with her snuggled up against me. We'd go out for a walk every afternoon in the fresh air and she'd sleep. I'd take her in the buggy but I'd have the sling with me so I could pop her in it if she seemed unhappy. I did the same with the others when they were little, too.'

Yvonne, mother of Anna, 6, Carla, 4, and Mia, 1 year

Buggies and car seats

Even if your baby spends a lot of time in a sling, there will almost certainly be occasions when he needs to go into some sort of travel seat, for example during a car journey, and most parents find they want to use a buggy for some situations, especially as their baby gets older.

The sort of pram or buggy you buy, and the way you set it up, can have a big impact on how keen your baby is to spend time in it. Some buggies can be switched round so the baby faces either forwards (away from their parent) or backwards (towards the parent), but others are fixed in one position only. Almost all young babies are happier if they can see their parent, even if they can't touch them, rather than looking outwards at unfamiliar places and fast-moving people, and research has shown that facing their parent helps the development of babies' language skills as well. Once they can sit up and turn themselves round to catch a glimpse of whoever is pushing them, older babies sometimes enjoy facing outwards,

Unexpected reactions

Babies become more aware of their surroundings as their focus broadens and they start to notice things they haven't really taken in before. Your baby may have been to your local shopping centre with you several times in the past but it's quite likely you'll find one day, for no apparent reason, that something about the bright lights, noise and crowds frightens him. This may also happen when he's been somewhere in a sling but then experiences it for the first time in a buggy, in which he may feel more vulnerable and from where the view is different. If possible, give him time to study anything new, and to touch things if he needs to, holding him all the while, so that his confidence is restored and he is ready to move on.

but being unable to see them can be frightening for a baby who is too young to know that someone hasn't disappeared forever when they are out of sight. This is especially relevant when the weather means the top and sides of the buggy have to be covered, making communication between parent and baby almost impossible. If you do use a forward-facing buggy, talk to your baby as you walk, and pop your head over the top every now and then so he can see your face, as this will help to reassure him. Make sure, too, that he can see you if you have to park the buggy with him in it. Whenever possible, let him guide you as to which way he wants to face, and be prepared for him to switch his preference from one to the other (and back again), as he grows.

The design of buggies and car seats can have implications for babies' health. For a baby who cannot sit up by himself, anything that encourages him to be in a slumped position, with his chin on his chest, is not good for his posture or his breathing. If your baby's buggy or car seat makes him adopt this position, it's best not to leave him in it longer than absolutely necessary. If the whole seat can be tilted back, this will allow him to breathe more easily but the angle of the seat against its base will still restrict the movement of his hip joints, which can end up fixed in one position for long periods of time.

Many parents find that a traditional-style pram – or the type of buggy that has a seat that goes completely flat – works better than a standard buggy (or a combo car seat buggy) while their baby is very young, because it allows him to sleep safely and comfortably for as long as he needs to. Older babies are often happier in a buggy like this, too, because it means they can sit up independently (secured by a harness) rather than being pinned against the back of the seat. In general, the more room and freedom your baby can have, the less likely he is to object to being strapped in, and the easier life will be for both of you.

Helping your baby adjust to a car seat

Some babies are quite happy to be put in a car seat; others object passionately but settle down once they're in it; still others seem to hate the whole experience (although they may still fall asleep in the seat once the car is in motion). Many go through phases of different levels of tolerance. Here are some tips for making car journeys with your baby as stress-free as possible for everyone:

• Try to allow plenty of time to settle your baby in his seat. Talk or sing to him at the same time.
• Invite his help to put on the straps, or make a game of it, so that he doesn't feel pulled about.
• For a younger baby, it may be easier to wait until he is in a deep sleep (see box on page 142) before transferring him to the car seat; make sure the car is reasonably warm, to help minimise the chances of him waking up.
• Try to have your baby's seat in a position where he can see you during the journey – a special baby car mirror may help if his seat is attached in the rear of the car.
• Talk or sing to your baby during the journey. Whenever it's safe, make eye contact with him.
• On long journeys, make a point of taking your baby out of his seat whenever you stop for a rest.
• Never leave your baby alone in the car, even if he's asleep. Waking up to find you're not there could be frightening for him.

'We kept Stan's buggy as a lie-flat pram until he was at least a year old – when he stretched right out he only just fitted into it. Most other babies we knew had their buggies as pushchairs by then, with a seat unit. But keeping the buggy flat meant Stan was never strapped into one position – he had a little harness and he could wriggle about and lie flat on his back or on his side. Once he could sit up he'd sit and play with his toys. He'd face us and we'd chat away with him – he was always happy to be in the buggy.'

Robyn, mother of Stan, 15 months

There are so many things that babies have no power over. They can't choose to opt out of a shopping trip, or decide when Granny will visit. And, until they are mobile, they have no say in where they sit, sleep or spend their time. Offering your baby the chance to choose, and explaining what you're doing when you're dressing him and taking him out, are important steps in helping him to develop a sense of who he is – and in helping him to feel he has some control over the things that happen to him.

Key points

- Everything you do with your baby is a chance for him to learn. Even repetitive activities can be made pleasurable and fun.
- Allowing your baby to make choices and participate in his care will mean basic tasks are more enjoyable – and resistance less likely.
- Getting to know your baby's body rhythms and signals will allow you to predict wees and poos and will encourage his transition to using the potty or toilet to happen naturally.
- Bathing isn't just about getting clean – bath time can be fun, especially if it's shared. And it's a great chance for your baby to learn about his body.
- Massage is a lovely way to communicate with your baby; it's calming for both of you.
- A sling is a great way to transport a baby, allowing him to sleep, feed or watch what's going on in comfort and

safety. Check your baby is well **HITCH**ed when you're carrying him this way.

- Being in a car seat or buggy will be more enjoyable for your baby if he can see and hear you as much of the time as possible.

10

Settling into parenthood

Becoming a parent involves dealing with some enormous changes and adapting your lifestyle to accommodate an additional person with needs that are very different from your own. This chapter is about adjusting to the reality of day-to-day life with your babe-in-arms, taking care of yourself and finding support for your new role. It's also about involving other people in your baby's care if you have to be apart from her, either for a few hours now and then, or on a regular basis.

So, is this it?

After the excitement and intensity of the first few weeks, many parents find themselves struggling to settle into their new life, especially if this is their first baby. Adjusting to being a parent can take longer than they expected, and many new mothers, in particular, continue to feel emotionally fragile or slightly disorientated for many weeks after the birth. Women who have had a particularly traumatic or difficult birth, or one that was very different from what they had imagined, may find it takes them several months to really feel they have recovered emotionally (see page 213 for more on this). Some aren't sure quite what's expected of them once the cards and flowers have stopped arriving and the visitors have been and gone. For many, the realisation that the baby is here to stay is itself hard to grasp.

'I found the first few months really difficult – I felt very down. Benjamin completely transformed my life, but I resisted the change and, in hindsight, that made it so much harder.'

Leah, mother of Benjamin, 11 months

Most babies are cared for primarily by one parent – usually their mother – for at least the first few months if not for years, while the other parent continues to work outside the home. It can be extremely hard to adapt to being the parent at home with a baby if you've had a busy working life before – whether or not you plan to go back to it. Some parents discover that they miss the structure and companionship of their working life, and feel a profound and unexpected sense of loss and loneliness as a result. Many parents at home in those first few months feel as if they are in limbo, waiting for life to get back to normal.

How this change affects you is likely to depend on the plans and expectations you had before your baby was born and how ready you were for something new. Most parents find life with their baby becomes easier once they recognise and accept that things will never be the same as they were before. This frees them up to begin to work out ways to adapt to their new role, to focus on the baby and to gain a sense of the kind of mother or father they are, or want to become.

'I remember meeting up with my antenatal group when Erin was about six weeks old and everyone seemed to be having such a hard time with their new babies. But I was really enjoying it. The first couple of months went by in a flash. I think the difference was that I was ready for my life to change – I didn't miss work at all and really enjoyed the new, slower pace.'

Francesca, mother of Erin, 7, Sophie, 4 years,
and Megan, 6 months

Some parents at home experience pressure to 'get back to normal', often from their friends and family, who may be keen to encourage them to organise a babysitter and go out for the evening, or appear to have made the assumption that they're looking forward to going back to work. They – and their friends – can be surprised if they discover that their priorities have changed and they no longer want to spend time doing the things they used to.

> 'There's a real expectation that you should just leave your baby and go out – but it's such a small amount of time when you can't do stuff. And there's so much pressure from the media to get your old life back – as though you are letting other women down if that's not what you want and that giving your child what they need is not enough. You're seen as "just a mother".'
>
> *Anna, mother of Tilly, 2 years*

You'll almost certainly find, as you settle into parenthood, that your ideas about what you can fit into a day will need a rethink. Trying to do all the things you used to do *and* look after a baby is unlikely to be realistic. Most new parents are amazed at how difficult it can be even to sit down together to eat a meal, never mind answer messages or keep the house tidy. Appointments that caused no problem in the past can suddenly be almost impossible to meet, with nappy changes, feeding and getting out of the house to manage first. It's easy to feel you'll never be able to cope. Many parents find that, once they begin to lower their expectations of what's possible, life becomes a bit easier. Setting small goals, ignoring the dust, and giving yourself a pat on the back for what you *have* achieved – rather than beating yourself up over what you didn't manage to do – can help each day seem more manageable. And it *does* get easier.

> 'I had Mickey all day from six months. He'd feed before Nicole left for work and we'd go off on our adventures. I really enjoyed being

in the park with him and seeing his sense of wonder at everything. Just doing the normal stuff with a baby takes up the whole day really. There were no schedules – I just followed his needs in terms of feeding and sleeping and the day seemed to schedule itself. All I did was to respond to what he wanted. As he got older it sort of grew organically – things just seemed to taper off and become something else. I just went with it.'

Ben, father of Mickey, 5 years, and Sam, 16 months

Looking after yourself

Being a parent is taxing and tiring – many new parents say it's the most difficult job they have ever done. So looking after yourself, as well as your baby, is important. If you constantly put your own needs last, everything can feel that much harder. Eating and drinking may not sound like something you'd forget, but it's all too easy to suddenly find it's four in the afternoon and you haven't had anything since breakfast. Making sure you have some quick and easy foods in the house so that you can grab something whenever you sit down to feed your baby will help you keep your energy levels up.

The traditional advice to nap when your baby naps, to make up for disturbed nights, can be useful, if not always easy to achieve when you have lots of other things to do (especially if you have older children). The alternative is to rush round catching up on chores while your baby is asleep. However, babies don't always need undivided attention when they are awake – they simply need to be close to one of their parents. This means that as long as your baby can see you and hear you easily, you may find she is quite happy watching while you get on with things. Some babies want their parents to chat to them, maybe about what they are doing, so they feel involved. Others (especially very young babies) just need to stay physically close to their mother or father, and will be happiest in a sling while he or she gets on with housework, gardening, DIY or shopping – or plays with the toddler. Your baby will let you know what she needs, and it may well be different on different days. Doing any essential chores while she is awake will free up time, so that (other children permitting) you can relax while she feeds and can catnap, if you need to, when she's asleep.

> 'I decided to prioritise being a mum over things like having a tidy house. It's that old saying – children grow up when you're not looking. So I'm a mum first and everything else second. I try to savour every moment – it goes so quickly.'
>
> *Emily, mother of Clara, 5, and Susy, 1 year*

Once you have a child, even simple things that you've probably taken for granted before, such as having a shower in the morning or going to the loo by yourself, may take a bit of planning. In general, doing things with your baby close to you – even when she's asleep – will probably work better than trying to snatch moments away from her. Mostly, she'll be more content if she's aware of your presence, and if she needs you to stop what you're doing you'll have plenty of warning. Many parents discover that running backwards and forwards every time their baby calls them from another room quickly becomes frustrating and tiring.

Some new parents find it helpful to work out what it is *they* need to do or have, in order to get through the day and still feel human at the end of it. For some it's fresh air or a bit of exercise; for others it's meeting other people or getting the washing-up done; or it might simply be having half an hour to read a book or enjoy a soak in the bath. Figuring out a way – perhaps with the help of your partner or a friend – to accommodate your baby's needs and fit in what *you* need as well may be enough to help you survive even the most difficult of days.

'When Alice was little, I'd only have a shower if she was asleep – but she'd only get to sleep if she was in the sling, outside in the fresh air. So I'd often be in our little front garden first thing in the morning, with her dressed and in the sling and me in my bathrobe, walking up and down to get her to sleep so I could have a shower.'

Martha, mother of Alice, 13 months

Adapting as a couple

Becoming parents, especially for the first time, will bring changes in your relationship. Some of these will probably be welcome but some will need to be negotiated, so that you can continue to support each other effectively. The unexpected emotions and new priorities that parenthood brings may mean that what you need from each other changes from day to day. Opportunities for sex may be less frequent and your keenness for it out of sync (it's easy to feel used up, both emotionally and physically, at the end of a full day of baby care). Talking to each other about how you are feeling may help to stop misunderstandings and resentment and enable you to share the joys *and* frustrations of parenting.

'I realised after a while you have to find time to be a couple too. If everything is hard work your relationship can get really stressful. You don't have to meet every single one of your baby's needs without considering your own needs too – it's a balance, and that balance is different for different people.'

Chantelle, mother of Madison, 14 months

Support from other people

It's not uncommon to feel isolated or abandoned when you're at home all day with a baby. This isn't surprising – humans evolved to live in groups, bringing up babies with their extended family around them, not on their own with almost no support. A newborn baby isn't great company, especially if she hasn't even discovered how to smile yet, and many parents find their relationship with their baby – and with each other – can become fraught if they are on their own with her for long periods. Spending time with other people can break up the intensity of life with a baby as well as providing a chance to share the ups and downs. And a day spent with someone who can help you recapture the looked-after feeling of a babymoon (see Chapter 4) can be an invaluable way to recharge your batteries when things get tough.

Grandparents, in particular, can be a welcome source of support. They have lots of experience to draw on and can help new parents to see their day-to-day struggles from a broader perspective. On the other hand, they may find it hard to adjust to their new role after the arrival of the baby. It's possible the whole family dynamic will need adjusting, something which can be difficult and often takes time. You may find that your parents or in-laws take a while to find the right balance between support and interference.

'It's a different kind of love with a grandchild. It's so special – you can enjoy the baby but you don't have the ultimate responsibility. If Penny cries I can comfort her without that panicky feeling you get as a new mum. And it's easy with my daughter – we are on the same wavelength and that really helps. She's doing things in a similar way to the way I did. Penny feeds when she wants and she's sleeping with her mum. There's no conflict, it's lovely. But my son's wife is expecting now and I know my daughter-in-law is planning to do things very differently, so we'll have to see how that goes.'

June, mother of two, grandmother of Penny, 7 weeks

When you're inexperienced, it's easy to doubt your own abilities; having someone who believes in you and tells you you're doing a good job can be the crucial ingredient that enables you to cope confidently. You may find this support is available from your family or old friends, but you might need to seek it out from others. Many new parents find enormous support from new friends, often those who are in a similar situation, with a baby of a similar age.

Getting out and meeting other people can often provide some structure to what may seem an endless round of feeding and changing, especially if it offers a chance to relax in an atmosphere of shared understanding. Going along to a local parent-and-baby group is one way to make new friends – although it may take a bit of 'try it and see' with a few different groups before you find one that suits you. This is especially true for stay-at-home dads – some areas have dedicated groups for fathers, although they are often held only at weekends. Being among people you feel comfortable with – even if you don't yet know them very well – can be hugely reassuring, especially if you're feeling under pressure to be the perfect parent.

'I went to a baby group, but the other mums were very different from me, with different expectations. Everyone was comparing what their babies did and how the parents had managed it. When I'd mention that Billy wouldn't settle in a buggy and was waking in the night, they'd say, "Poor you!" – so I thought it was a problem that I needed to do something about. When he was about four months I finally met some other mums who were more like-minded – I had found my tribe!'

Terry, mother of Billy, 8 months

Some areas have exercise groups, such as yoga, Pilates, swimming or jogging (with buggies) in the park, specifically for new mothers and babies, with the aim of combining toning up physically after the birth with getting out of the house and making new friends. If you're breastfeeding, you may find there's a local support group that meets regularly. Your midwife, health visitor, GP surgery, children's centre, sports centre or library will have details. Forums and social media are another great way to share experiences, and some offer the chance to meet up, as well as to chat online.

'The days were so long being stuck at home – I felt so isolated. When Charlotte was about six weeks I went to a baby massage group and made some really good friends. None of us had any family support nearby and we clung to each other. I found out how fantastic women can be for one another. I lived for those meetings.'

Maryanne, mother of Charlotte, 11 months

Dealing with unhelpful opinions

As a new parent, you'll probably find there's no shortage of people keen to tell you what you should be doing – especially if this is your first baby. From your friends and relatives to health professionals and bus drivers, it will sometimes seem as though everyone has an opinion to share. Some of what you hear will be useful, but some of it may leave you feeling confused, criticised, or as though you are doing everything wrong. As you get to know your baby your confidence will grow, but, in the meantime, it's worth having a few responses ready in case you need them.

'My sister-in-law gave me lots of advice, none of which I wanted to try. She meant well, though. I used to smile and say brightly, "Oh, that's an idea!"'

Natalia, mother of Peter, 6 months

Feeling low

The enormous emotional upheaval of the first few weeks of parenthood gradually diminishes for most parents, as their hormones stabilise (in the case of mothers) and they become more confident at looking after their baby. However, some parents – men and women – continue to feel down or unable to sleep, or find that negative feelings, such as worthlessness, hostility or a sense of being very distanced from their baby, surface later, after a brief period of emotional stability. This can signal postnatal depression.

Postnatal depression (or PND) varies in severity and can last for weeks or months. It most commonly affects mothers, but fathers can also suffer from it, although it may not always be recognised. Parents in this situation need support and help as soon as possible. It can be extremely difficult to talk about how you feel when you are depressed but PND is very common, and health professionals such as health visitors and family doctors are trained to look for the signs and provide referrals for further help. Options for treatment include counselling, psychotherapy, dietary supplements and anti-depressants. Relaxation techniques, fresh air and exercise can all be beneficial, too.

Input from family and friends can be enormously impor-tant for a parent suffering from PND, but it needs to be directed in a way that will be helpful in the long term as well as immediately. In general, practical support, such as help with housework, cooking and looking after older children, is likely to be most valuable; some parents want or need a break from their baby, but for others offers of help with baby care only compound feelings of uselessness and despair. Support to continue breastfeeding, if that's what the mother wants to do, can be particularly important, since she may feel it represents something unique that only *she* can do for her baby.

A common feature of PND is feeling unduly anxious, either about the baby or about being a parent, or feeling detached and unable to recognise the baby's needs or respond to her. Having someone with you to prompt you when your baby needs you – and reassure you when she doesn't – can help to keep your relationship with her responsive and calm.

'The anxiety I felt when Poppy was very little was paralysing. I could do basic practical things to keep going but I clung to her the rest of the time. Being physically close was incredibly important, even though I felt guilty crying in front of her. I wasn't sleeping and my parents came and took her out for half an hour so I could rest. But I was so tense without her – I just kept listening for her cry. The worst lasted a few weeks but it felt like forever. I thought it would always be a struggle.'

Carmen, mother of Poppy, 9 months

If you have experienced a difficult or traumatic birth, you may find yourself suffering symptoms not of depression but of post-traumatic stress disorder. These can include vivid flashbacks to the birth, as well as nightmares, anxiety and/or numbness. If you experience any symptoms that interfere with your ability to enjoy and care for your baby, contact your GP, so that he or she can refer you for treatment or counselling.

Managing separation

Some degree of separation happens to all babies and their parents sooner or later. Sometimes the process is entirely baby-led, when the baby shows she is happy to be cared for by someone else, but it can also happen because her main carer either wants or needs to be away, either for a few hours now and then or for much longer stretches, perhaps to go back to work or study.

Your baby is beginning to make relationships that extend beyond those closest to her the first time she smiles at someone other than you or your partner. From very early on, her world will include other people, from close friends and family, to strangers she encounters from the safety of your arms. The bond you and she are developing will offer her a safe place to come back to when she starts to move away of her own accord, or when she is separated by circumstances. However, her progress towards being happy when apart from you is likely to feel like two steps forward and one step back, with alternating bouts of confidence and neediness.

'Clinginess' is normal – and healthy

Very young babies can appear content to be cuddled by a variety of people but, at around five or six months, most suddenly start to become 'clingy'. Typically, you will notice your baby becoming acutely anxious if you move out of her line of sight, even for a few minutes. At around the same time she may start to refuse to be held by anyone she doesn't know well – and possibly even by anyone other than you. If you're not expecting it, the sudden appearance of this separation or stranger anxiety can be baffling, and may feel like a backward step. In fact, these behaviours are completely normal – it's their absence that isn't. They are a sign that your baby has developed a secure attachment to the most important people in her life and is beginning to understand that she can rely on you in a way that she daren't yet risk with anyone else.

The onset of clinginess is also a sign that your baby is developing a sense of time and distance, and of being a separate person from you. She is vaguely aware that, when you disappear from view, she doesn't know where you are or when you might be back. It's a genuinely scary situation for her, and her response is to want to hold on to you. Clinginess lasts, to some degree, well into the toddler years, although it gradually lessens in intensity. It is usually at its peak between about 6 and 18 months, which may seem strange, given that this is when babies appear to be so keen to strike out on their own. But clinginess and independence go hand in hand: the farther the baby finds herself from her parents (or the more scary the surroundings), the more she needs to touch base.

Babies need lots of reassurance during this phase if they are to develop true confidence to step out on their own.

Being baby-led is crucial to helping your baby to negotiate moving apart from you. Acknowledging her need to stay close to you at some times and not at others is key to helping her develop confidence and become self-reliant. Even if she was fine on her own in the kitchen for a few minutes last week, if she's not this week, expect to have to take her with you if you need to leave the room. If she seems nervous in the presence of a stranger, or won't go to someone that she used to trust, don't feel you have to force her to make closer contact than she wants to. If possible, let her go towards them, gradually, in your arms, rather than have *them* approach *her*.

A useful way to help your baby learn to trust you to come back is to explain what's happening if you need to go out of her sight briefly. For example, you might say, 'I'm just going to answer the door – I'll be back in a minute,' followed by, 'Here I am – back again.' You and your partner can do this for each other, too: 'Mummy's going to have a shower; she'll be back in 10 minutes … here she is – all nice and clean!' Babies get the gist of commonly repeated sentences well before they begin to speak, through associating them with whatever is happening at the time. Similarly, talking to your baby so she can continue to hear your voice while you are in a different room will help her learn that, although you're out of sight, you haven't abandoned her. Games of peek-a-boo and hiding are another way to help her understand that you are there even when she can't see you, and to become confident that you will reappear, should she need you.

Choosing a babysitter

If you need someone to care for your baby for a few hours, a family member or close friend who she knows well and trusts is likely to be your first choice. However, sometimes you may have to ask someone she is less familiar with, especially if you don't have much notice. In this case, it's important that the setting, at least, is familiar, so try to fix things so that the babysitter comes to your house rather than you taking your baby to theirs. If possible, arrange for them to come round for an hour or so the day before, so your baby can get to know them a little, and so that she will recognise them when she sees them again. You may want to do a practice run that day, leaving her with the babysitter for half an hour or so, so that she learns she can expect you to come back.

If meeting a day or two before isn't possible, try to make sure the sitter arrives well before you need to go out on the day itself, so that your baby has a chance to get used to their presence before she finds herself on her own with them. However much *you* trust the person who is looking after her, *she* needs to trust them, too – or to at least see that you do – if she is to feel safe. Arranging for the babysitter to come in advance will also give you an opportunity to explain to them some of the ways your baby tells you when she wants to feed, sleep or be cuddled. And, if she is used to being carried in a sling, you can show them how to use it. If she usually sleeps close to you at night she may need extra help to relax and fall asleep without you there, so passing on some of the soothing techniques that you've found work well for her will be helpful. (Make sure, though, that the babysitter knows she shouldn't be put into your bed on her own.)

Going back to work or study

As a general rule, the older a baby is when her main carer goes back to work or study, the easier the transition to having others share her care is for both of them. If you have a choice, the later you leave it, the stronger your baby's sense of security and belonging will be and the more able she'll be to cope with being apart from you. If you are breastfeeding, waiting until she is eight or nine months (or older, if you can) is likely to make a big difference, in particular to how much milk you need to express, because she will probably be eating some solid foods as well.

'I went back to work three days a week when Beth was six months, but it was awful. I was anxious about her – and I was no good at work because I was tired and distracted. With the commute we were apart for 10 hours – that's such a long day. So I felt I was doing both things badly. This time it's much easier. I waited until Molly was over eight months, work fewer hours and I don't have to travel, so we're only apart for six hours. It's made a huge difference.'

Samantha, mother of Beth, 5 years, and Molly, 13 months

Choosing the type of care that you want for your baby while you're at work may be time-consuming and challenging, so it's a good idea to start planning it well in advance. Some parents find that informal, more traditional childcare arrangements can work very well – for example, with grandparents or other family members looking after the baby, or sharing childcare with a friend who has a baby of a similar age. Others prefer to use a nanny, childminder or nursery. Whoever looks after your baby, it's important that they understand and share your approach to parenting – if it's someone you don't know well, try asking them how they would deal with some hypothetical situations. It will help, too, if the person or place you choose is able to make a long-term commitment to caring for your child, so that she doesn't have to get used to a series of different people.

Ideally, your baby's substitute care will be as close as possible to what she is used to at home. Being with a nanny, who will look after her in your house, or with a childminder in *their* home, is likely to feel safer to her than the larger and more crowded environment of a nursery. This is a particularly important consideration while she's under a year old. If a nursery is the only realistic option for you, try to find one where there is a higher than normal ratio of staff to children, a low staff-turnover rate and a strong commitment to responsive, loving care. The presence of members of staff who will cuddle your child if she is distressed will have a greater impact on her well-being than, for example, the quality of the play equipment, or the nutritional value of the snacks. Spending some time at the nursery over several sessions (either with or without your baby), so that you can meet and observe different members of staff, will help you decide whether it's the right place for your baby.

> 'Lottie, our first child, was about four months when I went back to work full-time. She went to a lovely, small nursery very close to my office. Eight hours a day in nursery sounds a lot but she spent the other 16 with me. Sometimes we'd meet a friend for a drink afterwards; other times we'd just go home, have tea and chill out in front of the TV, cuddling and feeding.'
>
> *Donna, mother of Lottie, 10, Martha, 8, Ashley, 4, and Amy, 2 years*

Many parents' first thought is to look for childcare near to where they live. However, if you commute to work, finding someone close to your workplace may make more sense; it will cut down the time you and your baby are apart and may also work out cheaper, because she'll be there for fewer hours. If you are breastfeeding, having her cared for nearby will mean the gap between her last feed before you have to leave her and her first feed when you get back is as short as possible, saving you time expressing milk and making it less likely that you will get uncomfortably full while at work. If she is really close by, you may even be able to pop in to feed her during your lunch hour.

If you are apart from your baby for most of the day, expect her to need to catch up on cuddles when you get home. If you are breastfeeding she is likely to want to go straight to the breast when she sees you. She may well need extra feeding and cuddle-time on your non-working days, too. Many parents find that sleeping as close as possible to their baby allows them to make up for time spent apart and helps to recharge their relationship with her, even while they sleep. (See page 150 for more on bed sharing and safe sleeping.)

'I went back to work when Lucy was eight months. I wasn't looking forward to it, but because we were still breastfeeding, and Lucy was sharing our bed, we stayed close. So I've never felt I missed out on parenting.'

Carlotta, mother of Lucy, 4 years

Keeping breastfeeding going when you're apart

Depending on her age, if your baby is with someone else for longer than an hour or two she may need you to leave her some expressed breastmilk or formula. (For information

Storing breastmilk

You can store expressed breastmilk in a feeding bottle, a specially designed sterile bag, or a food-safe plastic container that has been thoroughly sterilised (cleaned and then scalded with boiling water). It can be kept safely at normal room temperature for up to six hours, and for about eight hours in a cool bag with ice packs. If you need to keep it for longer than this, a domestic fridge will be fine for about three days (up to eight days if the temperature stays below 4°C/39°F) and a freezer for six months. Frozen breastmilk should be defrosted slowly, if possible, and used immediately. There's no need to heat it before it's offered to your baby but, if she prefers it warm, standing it in a jug of hand-hot water for a minute or two is safer than using a microwave.

on expressing, contact a breastfeeding supporter – via one of the breastfeeding support organisations, see 'Sources of Information and Support', page 229 – or your health visitor.) Freezing small amounts of breastmilk occasionally will mean you'll always have some available at short notice, and having a small stock to fall back on will give you peace of mind if you and your baby are going to need to be apart repeatedly.

> 'It was hard going back to work – Dylan was just six months. Every time I thought about him I'd have a rush of milk – I always had to have loads of breast pads with me. A guy at work had five kids who'd all breastfed and he organised a room and space in the fridge for me for expressing. But I didn't bother with the room – I'd just pump for 10 minutes in the loo a couple of times a day. And when I got home Dylan would be feeding almost before I'd got my coat off.'
>
> Ava, *mother of Dylan, 1 year*

Some breastfed babies will happily accept milk from a bottle or cup but some are resistant to feeding any other way than at the breast. If this is the case with your baby, offering her a bottle before she is truly hungry may work, or you could try letting her play with the bottle so she can figure out what it is for herself. However, if she refuses to take milk from whoever is looking after her, it's safe to respect her choice. Babies don't starve themselves; if she needs food she'll take it. Either way, if you let her breastfeed as much as she wants in the evening and during the night you will help her to deal with her hunger *and* reconnect with you.

You will be at the centre of your baby's world for a long time. Even as she begins to leave the safety of your arms, crawling off on her own to explore her surroundings and meet new people, she will continue to need you as her safe haven – a secure base to come back to, to recharge her batteries – for several years. Allowing yourself to be baby-led from the beginning will give you and your baby a strong foundation on which to build. It will make navigating the gradual ending of the in-arms phase of babyhood easier and smoother for both of you, enabling you to embrace toddlerhood, and all it has to offer, with confidence and anticipation.

Key points

- Finding a new life as a parent is challenging – but it does get easier. The secret is to be ready to adapt, reassess what you can achieve in a day, take things gradually – and be gentle with yourself and your partner, just as you are with your baby.
- It's important not to overlook your own well-being while focusing on caring for your baby.
- Your wider family may be a welcome source of support for you in your new role.
- Sharing experiences with other new parents can help you adjust to your new way of life. Local groups and social media may help you take the plunge.
- Postnatal depression is not uncommon. If you're finding parenthood difficult, ask for help.
- Clinginess is normal – and healthy. You are your baby's safe haven, to which she needs to be able to return frequently, as new people and places become part of her life.
- Choose carefully the people who will share your baby's care, and help her to negotiate the challenge of being apart from you gradually and gently.

Conclusion

Parenthood can be exciting, frustrating, puzzling, exhausting and a source of joy and wonder, often all at the same time, and it can be hard to imagine how your life with your baby will unfold. What you can be sure of is that his need for you will evolve as he grows – but that it will never be greater than while he is a babe in arms.

The key to baby-led parenting is staying in touch with your baby and doing what feels right for him, and seems to keep him happy. No individual can be guaranteed a lifetime of happiness, but if your child is listened to and knows he is loved as an infant this solid foundation will foster an inner sense of his own self-worth and provide a buffer for life's blows. We hope this book has given you the confidence to trust your baby – and yourself – to know what's best for him, so that you can be the parent he needs you to be. Whether it's feeding, bathing, playing or sleeping, he knows what he needs and how to ask for it; he just needs you to respond to what he's telling you.

As your baby begins to move away from you his needs will change, but the relationship you have built during his most vulnerable months will help you to adapt and move with him. Continuing to talk with your partner throughout your baby's childhood – and being prepared to amend your approach if it doesn't appear to be working – will keep you on track as your child grows.

Expect to revisit previous decisions when siblings come along and challenge you in new and different ways. If you need to change tack, try to be gentle with yourself and each other, rather than beating yourselves up. Children are resilient – they can bounce back from difficult episodes, provided that something that isn't working isn't repeated over and over. And don't forget to give yourselves a pat on the back occasionally. Parenting isn't easy, but it can be *very* rewarding.

We wish you well on your parenting journey.

Sources of information and support

We recommend the following websites as just a few of the many resources available to support parents in the UK.

General parenting support and information

Best Beginnings campaigns to give every baby the healthiest possible start in life.
www.bestbeginnings.org.uk

Bliss provides support and care to premature and sick babies and their families.
www.bliss.org.uk

Born Ready is one of several websites providing information about not using nappies, also known as elimination communication.
www.bornready.co.uk

The Fatherhood Institute works to produce a society in which all children have a strong and positive relationship with their father and any father-figures.
www.fatherhoodinstitute.org

ISIS (Infant Sleep Information Source) provides information about normal infant sleep based upon the latest UK and worldwide research.
www.isisonline.org.uk

Maternity Action aims to promote the health and well-being of all pregnant women, their partners and children.
www.maternityaction.org.uk
Telephone helpline: 0845 600 8533

Mumsnet is currently the UK's biggest network for parents.
www.mumsnet.com

Netmums is a general information forum run by mums in conjunction with health professionals.
www.netmums.com

The NCT provides general information on birth and parenting.
www.nct.org.uk

Support for parents of multiples

The Multiple Births Foundation aims to improve care and support for multiple birth families.
www.multiplebirths.org.uk

The Twins and Multiple Births Association (Tamba) aims to help parents meet the unique challenges of multiple birth.
www.tamba.org.uk

Advice and information on slings

Babywearing UK is a social enterprise which aims to promote the use of slings and baby carriers, to share the benefits for parents and babies and to help all parents access support via sling meets, libraries and trained babywearing consultants.
www.babywearing.co.uk

SlingGuide is a comprehensive, independent site run by volunteers who want to help others choose and use a sling which is best for them.
www.slingguide.co.uk

Support and information about infant feeding

National helplines

The UK has four **mother-to-mother support** organisations, each offering support and information about breastfeeding and a national telephone helpline. Some also offer local one-to-one support and group get-togethers. The BfN provides specialist information on drugs in breastmilk. These organisations are not equally active in all areas of the UK but it's likely one of them will have a group near you.

The Association of Breastfeeding Mothers (ABM)
http://abm.me.uk
National helpline: 0300 330 5453

The Breastfeeding Network (BfN)
www.breastfeedingnetwork.org.uk
National helpline: 0300 100 0210

La Leche League GB (LLLGB)
www.laleche.org.uk
National helpline: 0845 120 2918

The NCT (National Childbirth Trust)
www.nct.org.uk
National helpline: 0300 330 0700

The NHS National Breastfeeding Helpline is staffed by volunteers from some of the above groups: 0300 100 0212

Additional feeding resources

The Baby Café™ charity co-ordinates a network of breast-feeding drop-in centres run by health-care practitioners and voluntary breastfeeding counsellors.
www.thebabycafe.org

The Breastfeeding Welcome Scheme aims to support mothers' right to breastfeed their babies when they are out and about. The website gives details of businesses and venues in various areas across the UK that have signed up to welcome breastfeeding.
www.breastfeedingwelcomescheme.org.uk

First Steps Nutrition Trust provides independent information about formula milks, as well as other matters relating to nutrition from pre-conception to five years.
www.firststepsnutrition.org

The UNICEF UK Baby Friendly Initiative works with the health-care system to ensure high standards of care for pregnant women, mothers and babies. You can find out from the UNICEF website whether or not your local hospital or community trust has a Baby Friendly award. This site is also an excellent source of up-to-date information and research on breastfeeding.
http://live.unicef.org.uk/babyfriendly

Support for working parents

Acas (Advisory, Conciliation and Arbitration Service) aims to improve organisations and working life through better employment relations. It offers support to employers and employees and produces a booklet 'Accommodating breast-feeding employees in the workplace'.
www.acas.org.uk
Telephone helpline: 0300 123 1100

Childcare.co.uk is a good place to start if you need any form of child care.
www.childcare.co.uk

The Health and Safety Executive produces a leaflet 'A guide for new and expectant mothers who work'.
www.hse.gov.uk/mothers

Maternity Action offers advice for parents and employers about parents' rights at work, and to benefits and healthcare. It has a range of publications and information sheets.
www.maternityaction.org.uk
Advice line: 0845 600 85 33

Working Families aims to help working parents achieve a good balance between their responsibilities at home and at work.
www.workingfamilies.org.uk

About the authors

Gill Rapley has worked as a midwife and a health visitor. She has also been a voluntary breastfeeding counsellor and lactation consultant. More recently, she spent 14 years working for the UNICEF UK Baby Friendly Initiative. She and her husband have three grown-up children and live in Kent.

Tracey Murkett is a writer and journalist; she is also a voluntary mother-to-mother breastfeeding helper. She lives in London with her partner and their daughter, now aged nine.

Gill and Tracey are the authors of *Baby-led Breastfeeding: How to make breastfeeding work with your baby's help*, *Baby-led Weaning: Helping your baby to love good food* and *The Baby-led Weaning Cookbook*.

Acknowledgements

We would like to thank everyone whose suggestions, comments and wisdom have helped us to put this book together, and all the parents who shared their stories with us. We are particularly grateful to Claire Davis, Carmel Duffy, Jessica Figueras, Rebecca Harvey, Hazel Jones and Charlotte Russell for valuable feedback on the early manuscript and for insight, support and inspiration.

Thanks, also, to our editors, Sam Jackson and Louise Francis, for their patience and tolerance, to our agent, Clare Hulton, for her unfailing support, and to our long-suffering families for putting up with the late nights and for supplying endless cups of tea.

Index

Also available from Vermilion
by Gill Rapley and Tracey Murkett:

Baby-led Weaning

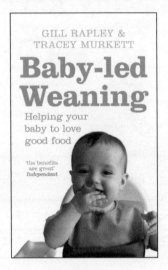

Baby-led Weaning is a practical and authoritative guide to introducing solid food the baby-led way. Through following your baby's natural skills and instincts, you can enable him to grow up a happy and confident eater.

With practical tips for getting started and the low-down on what to expect, *Baby-led Weaning* explodes the myth that babies need to be spoon-fed and shows why self-feeding from the start is the healthiest way for your child to develop.

Baby-led weaning is a common-sense, safe, easy and enjoyable approach to feeding your baby. No more purées and weaning spoons, and no more mealtime battles. Simply let your baby feed himself healthy family food.

£10.99   ISBN 9780091923808

Order this title direct from www.randomhouse.co.uk

The Baby-led Weaning Cookbook

In *Baby-led Weaning*, Gill Rapley and Tracey Murkett introduced parents to a common-sense, easy and enjoyable approach to starting solid foods. Now *The Baby-led Weaning Cookbook* offers a range of simple recipes for nutritious meals that the whole family can share, helping to make your child a happy and confident eater.

Full of healthy, delicious meal ideas and beautifully illustrated throughout, *The Baby-led Weaning Cookbook* also includes:

- simple advice on getting started
- essential at-a-glance information on nutrition and food safety
- ideas for quick snacks and lunches as well as desserts and family dinners
- anecdotes and quotes from parents

The Baby-led Weaning Cookbook will give parents the confidence to create exciting and enjoyable mealtimes, allowing their baby to develop his skills as he progresses with food.

£12.99 ISBN 9780091935283

Order this title direct from www.randomhouse.co.uk

Baby-led Breastfeeding

This straightforward and practical guide shows you how to follow your baby's lead so you can enjoy relaxed and pain-free breastfeeding.

Discover how to:

- help your baby follow his instincts from the very first feed
- make the most of the first few weeks to get breastfeeding up and running
- hold your baby in ways that will help him to feed effectively
- recognise when breastfeeding is going well and be confident that your baby is getting plenty of breast milk
- avoid common problems – from sore nipples to mastitis

Baby-led Breastfeeding is a sensible and sensitive guide that will help you and your baby develop a happy and fulfilling breastfeeding relationship.

£10.99 ISBN 9780091935290

Order this title direct from www.randomhouse.co.uk